CHANGEABILITY

CHANGEABILITY

MANAGE YOUR MIND – CHANGE YOUR LIFE

KATHRYN BRYANT

A Step-by-Step Mind Management Programme
to Create the Life You Want

Published by Brilliant Living® (find us at http://www.brilliantlivinghq.com)

Copyright © Kathryn Bryant 2014.

For information please contact Kathryn Bryant through http://www.brilliantlivinghq.com or by email at Hello@BrilliantLivingHQ.Com

First published July 2014

All material in this book is provided for information or educational purposes only. No content is intended to be a substitute for professional medical advice, diagnosis or treatment.

Contents

INTRODUCTION

"Your life does not get better by chance, it gets better by change." ~ Jim Rohn

WHY I WROTE THIS BOOK

It started on a damp February morning.

I was stuck in traffic and late for the meeting I'd just driven 150 miles to get to.

"*Go Go Go*", I screamed at the car ahead as he let someone into the queue. I knew I was totally overreacting but I didn't care. I was utterly fed up and frustrated.

The radio news at the top of the hour meant the meeting had started. Right now my colleagues were hearing about the restructure of our organization. Any minute the rumoured office move would be confirmed and everyone would be frantically thinking through the implications for them. As I sat there I did the same. Waiting for the traffic to move I calculated the hours I spent in my car in a week, a month, a year, and the impact of the 140 mile daily round trip to the new office. It all added up to a lot of life.

As the newsreader signed off with the weather, more rain, and the date, I was momentarily transported back to this day 8 years earlier. A day which started like any other but ended with the hit and run that cut short my father's life, and caused the stress and illness that hastened my mother's death 3 years later. Was that why I felt so out of sorts today?

I don't know if it was the poignancy of the anniversary, the frustration of the traffic, the prospect of yet another reorganization and more driving, or just the miserable grey drizzle, but in that instant the unacknowledged question I had held at bay, leapt into my consciousness and confronted me. 'Is this it? Is this as good as it gets. Is this what you want for the next twenty years until retirement, or could there be more?

I'm not someone who's given to dramatic emotional outbursts; indeed I was a world expert at bouncing back and getting on with it. And I knew I had much to be thankful for. I was fit and healthy and had a nice life; great husband, wonderful son, decent house and adorable dog. I had a good job (secure, well paid and mostly rewarding) and was a successful achiever who'd loved my job, even if the good bits gradually got less and the frustrations got more.

But I knew about the fragility of life, how it was short and none of us knew how short. It certainly wasn't something I normally dwelled on but the questions lingered. 'Is this how I want to be spending my precious time? Are these the experiences I want to be having?'

And although I didn't realize it at the time, sitting in that car in that moment, was the start of a process.

A process that saw me rethink my priorities and what I wanted – more flexibility and control over my time, more freedom and creative ways to use my skills and experience. And led me to change my work from Director in a Government organization to co-founder of BrilliantLivingHQ.com.

With the change in job came a change in lifestyle. Now my day starts with a walk by the river with my dog (who much prefers this new setup). Instead of an hour and a half in the car, my commute is twenty stairs to the office at the top of the house or wherever I fancy taking my laptop, to experience the roller coaster excitement and challenges of running my own show. Life isn't perfect but I love it and feel like I have my life back. I do the work I want in the way that suits me. This might mean staying up all night because I'm in the flow and it doesn't matter what time I get up in the morning, or having a leisurely lunch with my husband to talk about our next project. In short I have more of the time, creativity, flexibility and freedom that I realized I longed for.

But this book isn't about me; it's about you. For me it was my work I wanted to change, for you it might be something else. Something that makes you feel, 'If only I could change this, my life would be better.'

Whatever it is you want to change or improve in your life, if you don't do something to make that change then it's probably not going to happen (or not in the way you want). And you're going to wake up in 1, 2, 5, 10 or 20 years time wondering if this is it or could there be more, and wishing you'd made that change now, and neither of us want that.

So I wrote this book to share a way to make that change happen for you. It's called *Changeability*, because it's about developing your *Change-Ability*, the ability to change, so you can live the life you want.

But you know from experience that change isn't easy.

We've all tried to change things in our lives and failed, (diets, fitness regimes, habits). Or decided at New Year or a birthday that this year will be different, only for it to turn into a repeat of the past. Or worse still didn't even try because we thought we couldn't do it and settled for second best (job, partner, location, income).

'If you don't like it – change it' may be simple to say but not so simple to do. Change can be hard. But it doesn't have to be. You see it's not your fault. Change is supposed to be difficult because that's how we're programmed to be. Yet once you understand that programming and how to work with it, you have a way to increase your success in whatever you want to do.

This book gives you an understanding of that programming and ways to manage it.

It's based on three things – personal experience, study and research, and over twenty years of helping people change through education and training.

Throughout this time I looked at tactics, tools and techniques to help people change, and what holds them back and how to get past the barriers. One of the most important things I came to understand is that most barriers and the means to overcome them are connected to our minds.

You can have all the techniques and tactics you want but if your mind isn't set for change it means almost nothing. Likewise you can spend ages developing your mind and ways of thinking but if you don't have tactics for doing something with it, you'll not actually change or achieve anything.

I saw the limitations of great business tools like goal setting, when they ignore the personal aspect like people's motivation, internal beliefs and expectations. While at the other end of the spectrum I saw the tantalising focus on thought and mind in new age practices like the law of attraction, frustrated by a lack of action and clarity over what to actually do.

What was needed was a way to manage the mind combined with tactics for change.

So I set out to merge the best change and mind management techniques into one coherent step-by-step programme, and to make it comprehensive but not long, straightforward but not dumbed down, practical and easy to follow.

It was like doing a massive jigsaw puzzle with pieces spread across different subjects, programmes, websites and books (there's over 6000 books on Amazon about change). Different perspectives meant the pieces didn't quite fit together. So I took those pieces, the most important themes, theories and techniques, tested them, understood how they related to each other and how to fit them together for optimum results. This book is the result.

As someone who likes to understand how and why something works, it was important to show the rationale behind the techniques and how they slot together. Not least because experience shows we achieve best when we understand why we're doing something and have a step-by-step approach to what we're doing.

Like ingredients in a recipe the techniques are not unique, but the way they're put together and what I've done with them is my recipe and contribution. I've brought together ten powerful techniques from the worlds of personal development, psychology, neuroscience, business, sport, entertainment and spirituality and woven them into a logical integrated practical process. Where each step builds on the previous one but remains valuable in its own right.

WHY YOU SHOULD READ THIS BOOK

> *"He had to admit that the biggest inhibitor to change lies within yourself, and that nothing gets better until you change."* ~ Spencer Johnson, M.D.

The short answer is if you want to change something in your life, you should read this book because it shows you a smart way to do it.

It might be one particular thing that's keeping the life you want just out of reach, or you might want a whole lifestyle makeover. You might have a nice life with lots to be thankful for but feel there should be more and want to take it to the next level.

You might want to improve your focus, productivity, confidence; have more money, friends, fun, time, expertise, skills, promotion, a new career, write a book, start a new business, travel the world, find new love or improve your relationship, release your creativity, become a slimmer, fitter, healthier you or experience more happiness.

Whatever it is you want to change, the beauty of the *Changeability* programme is it's a framework you can apply to change it.

Specifically you should read this book:

- If you want to know exactly what to do to create the right mindset to take charge of your life and change what you don't like into what you do like.
- If you want to harness the power of your mind to overcome self-sabotage and help you get what you want.
- If you're busy with living so prefer to read one short book instead of 10 long ones.
- If you want everything in one place in an easy to follow format that suits your busy lifestyle.
- If you want to save time, money and energy, shorten your learning curve and the path to your success.
- If you want just enough theory to understand what you're doing and why, all explained in a straightforward logical way.
- If you want a 10-step framework of clear practical steps you can put into action straight away.
- If you want to master life enhancing techniques and skills you can use for the rest of your life to get the most out of life.

In short, you should read this book if you want a concise one-stop shop of everything you need to change and start creating a life you love today.

It doesn't matter what age you are or what stage of life you're at. It doesn't matter whether you want to change one thing or many things. Within you lies the power and ability to change, and this book shows you how.

This is not a get rich quick book, nor a book about magic or waiting for the universe to deliver. If that's what you're after then this is not the book for you. However you can use it to change your income, some of it may seem to work like magic, and there are similarities with elements of the law of attraction, but it's much more than that. It's a practical guide of powerful ways to manage your mind and improve your life.

Can I promise you a life of riches, fulfilling relationships and never-ending happiness? Of course not, no one can guarantee you that. But I can show you tried and tested methods to use in a systematic way to get what you want, if you choose to take action. Follow this carefully planned sequence of techniques and tools and you will change. If you read, understand and carry out the powerful practical actions, you will manage your mind and change your life.

WHAT YOU WILL KNOW BY THE END OF THIS BOOK

By the end of this book:

- You will have created your vision of brilliant living. Brilliant living is shorthand to describe life after you've changed what you want to change, and is personal to you.
- You will know what's been stopping you reaching your goals and how to change it.
- You'll have cleared the thoughts and beliefs that get in the way of your brilliant life and replaced them with empowering positive ones that help rather than hinder you.

- You'll understand the powerful technique that leading athletes and performers use to get to the top of their game and know how to use it to take your life to the next level.
- You'll know how to get the most out of every day and be the happiest you can be now.
- You will have experienced the key method used by millions of people throughout the world to improve their focus, understanding and life in general.
- You will be open to new opportunities to help you change that previously passed you by.
- You will have the energy, focus and impetus to take inspired action every day.
- You will understand what to do to keep good things happening for you.
- You will be changing your life and celebrating big time.

HOW TO USE THIS BOOK

In *Part 1 – The Changeability Backstory,* the concepts and context behind the *Changeability* programme are introduced. This gives you the background to understanding the actions of Part 2.

In *Part 2 – The Changeability Programme,* you get down to the business of change as you're guided through 10 steps and techniques to manage your mind and change your life. Each step has explanations interspersed with practical actions to work through.

If you want to get started really quickly, at the end of each chapter you'll find a quick start action you can do in five minutes. This is one thing you can do straight away to get going with that technique. You will of course get the best value from doing all the actions, but I really recommend that at the very least, you do this quick start one.

I've kept the book as short as possible to give you the minimum information required for maximum effectiveness, without the fluff. I suggest you read it through once and then return to the beginning of Part 2 to do the actions.

Endnotes and references can be found at the end of the book.

YOUR ACTION WORKSHEETS

A free workbook of action worksheets is available for you to download at http://www.BrilliantLivingHQ.com/ changeabilityws to accompany Part 2. These are in Word format to complete on your computer, or print out if you prefer writing by hand (as I like to do when thinking something through).

At the end of the book you'll find a summary guide to all of the techniques and actions. You may find this a useful tool to keep track of where you are, what you're doing and why you're doing it!

ARE YOU READY TO CHANGE YOUR LIFE?

Most people do not like change. They might think they want it but when it actually comes down to it they're fearful of things being different (there are sound reasons for this to take into account when making changes, which we go into later).

By virtue of the fact you're reading this you're already ahead of the crowd. And when you've successfully accomplished it, your life will never be the same.

Your idea of what you want to change and what turns living into brilliant living is unique to you. *Changeability* is about making your life the life you want it to be. This programme is for you – for your life on your terms, with the only limit being the limit of your imagination and the power of your action.

This is your moment, your time to step into the spotlight, to change what you want to change and create the life you want.

So get ready to read, think, dream, write, imagine, act and change your life.

part 1

THE CHANGEABILITY BACKSTORY

1. YOUR CHANGED LIFE

"When I was 17, I read a quote that went something like: 'If you live each day as if it was your last, someday you'll most certainly be right.' It made an impression on me, and since then, for the past 33 years, I have looked in the mirror every morning and asked myself: 'If today were the last day of my life, would I want to do what I am about to do today?' And whenever the answer has been 'No' for too many days in a row, I know I need to change something."
~ Steve Jobs

Changing your life and creating the life you want doesn't just happen by chance. It's not down to luck or even circumstance. It depends on making the conscious decision to change what you want to change to get the life you want, and making it happen.

THE FIRST STEP

Getting from where you are now to where you want to be is like travelling from A to B.

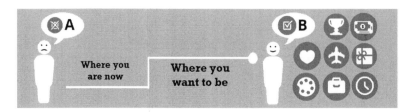

Sounds simple doesn't it? Well it certainly helps if you know where you are and where you want to be. But the truth is that most people don't, or only have a vague idea.

What about you? I'm guessing that because you've made the wise decision to read this, you're interested in changing or improving something in your life, so you've made it to the starting blocks.

A good place to start is to think about what 'B' means to you and what you need to change to get there. 'B' is how you want your life to be. This is your life after you've changed what you want to change.

Here are some ideas about what you might want to do in your changed life.

- Spend more time with your family and favourite people.
- Be financially secure with no worries about how to pay the next bill.
- Take exotic holidays abroad.
- Get a promotion or a new job or career.
- Be slim, healthy and fit.

- Find the perfect partner or improve your relationship with the one you've got.
- Feel excited about the future.
- Start your own business.
- Support your favourite causes.
- Live in a penthouse apartment in the city, a log cabin by a lake or a house on the beach.
- Plant a beautiful garden or grow vegetables on an allotment.
- Work from a laptop on the beach.
- Master a musical instrument.
- Write your first novel.
- Spend time on your favourite hobby or start a new one.
- Have lots of fun.
- Be enthusiastic for life.
- Own lots of fast cars? Have a manservant named Jeeves?

Maybe some of these resonated with you. One of the things that went through my mind when I started out on my *Changeability* journey was that I wanted to go to bed and get up when I felt like it. It might seem trivial, but as a night person, having to get up early every day to get to meetings or the office was a constant source of irritation. For me 'B' in this respect meant having the freedom to organize my time as I wished and a lifestyle without the Sunday night / Monday morning feeling, but where everyday had that Saturday feeling.

Here are some questions to help you think about what your 'B' looks like:

- What did you dream of doing when you were a child?
- What would you do if you had a million pounds?
- What would you do if you knew you couldn't fail?

Don't worry about the detail for now, this is just to start you thinking about the life you want and what you're going to change to get there. In part 2 we'll go through a way of capturing these desires to turn them into goals and actions. For now I just want to make the point that it's important to have a clear vision of what your changed life looks like, whether it's a small change like a habit or a bigger lifestyle change, because this vision will form the basis of your goals.

Your vision and goals can be one and the same, but it's useful to see goals as a way of breaking up or articulating parts of your vision. Goals are like mini-visions that help you see a clear path.

Experience shows that having goals based on your desires is crucial for making changes in your life. It might sound like stating the obvious, but it's hard to overestimate the importance of your goals, as they represent the destination you want to get to.

A WALK OR A JOURNEY?

If you don't know where you're going how will you know if you are on the right track or when you get there? It's like the difference between going for a walk and going on a journey. For a journey there may be many ways of getting there with distractions along the route, but the point is you need to know the destination so you can go in the general direction.

It doesn't mean there's only one mode of transport, or one correct route or timescale. In other words you're not shutting down your options but rather ensuring you're going in the right direction.

However it's dressed up, goal setting is a key feature of all self and personal development. Ever since the British philosopher and industrial psychologist Cecil Alec Mace conducted the first experimental studies of goal setting in 1935, and Edwin A. Locke further developed the theory in the 1960s, goal setting has been used as a motivational tool.

An army of human resources personnel have devised myriad ways of setting, monitoring and evaluating goals (or objectives in the vocabulary of the workplace). Goal setting is a vital component of sports psychology and coaching to enhance sporting performance. It's a key element in business and personal coaching and mentoring, and a cornerstone of group support networks like study or mastermind groups.

There may be differences around the details of goal setting, (specific, developmental, short-term, long-term etc.), but it's striking how often the practice of setting goals features not only in personal development but also in the life stories of successful people.

If you find the language of goals off-putting (too reminiscent of performance reviews and work objectives) then think of them in terms of aspirations, aims or ambitions.

Goals or aspirations or whatever you choose to call them are really just a means of capturing and specifying aspects of what you want your brilliant life to look like and what needs to change to get you there.

WHAT IS STOPPING YOU GETTING WHAT YOU WANT?

So you've given some initial thought to the changes you'd like to make, and your desires and the goals or aspirations you will soon be setting. You understand the idea that goal setting is an effective tool. Yet is there a *'BUT'* lingering in your mind? If so you won't be alone.

- BUT there must be a lot more to it than this – if it's this easy why isn't everyone doing it?
- BUT I could never achieve what I really want so I thought about something that didn't seem way out of reach for me.
- BUT I've seen *'The Secret'* and read about 'The Law of Attraction' and sat back and waited for the universe to deliver and am still waiting.
- BUT I've set goals in the past and always given up before I achieve them.

So what is stopping you?

2. **YOUR STARTING POINT**

A city fellow is lost in the darkest depths of the countryside trying to find the way to his hotel. He sees a local chap leaning on a fence chewing straw (you get the picture!). In desperation he pulls over to ask him directions. The local looks at him for a moment whilst pondering his question, sucks his teeth and replies in a characteristic rural tone, 'Yes I can – but I wouldn't start from here if I was you.'

The point of this old story is it's not just about where you want to be heading that's important, but where you're starting from as well. Like the lost man, your starting point is where it is, end of story.

So to get from A to B, you have to know where you are going to (life after change) but you also need to know where you are starting from and the potential hazards and road blocks along the way.

This is the step most people miss out, but don't do that because your starting point is a vital component of this system. It holds the key to understanding why you've struggled to achieve goals in the past, and therefore why and how to do things differently from now on.

So where are you starting from? While the details of individual circumstances will vary enormously there are likely to be common themes and characteristics.

THE EVERYDAYNESS OF LIFE

For most of us the starting point is what I call the 'everydayness' of life. Ranging from the daily routine of doing all the things that make our lives work (going to work, packing up lunch, doing our washing), to feeling utterly overwhelmed and exhausted by our commitments and the demands on us, and everything in between. This might be compounded by a lack of money or skills, or a shortage of time to put in the effort to make changes and achieve your goals.

All of this and more may represent your starting point, yet the biggest impact on where you are coming from can't be seen. It is going on inside your head and is all about your thoughts, beliefs and habits.

YOUR BELIEFS AND HABITS

We all carry round views about the world and ourselves in our heads. The way we view ourselves is built up from many sources over the course of our life, often coming from what people said to us. Over time we believe this is what we are like. With repetition from others and ourselves these beliefs become habits in terms of the way we think and act. In due course we begin to think of them as the truth or the facts as we see them.

The basis of these beliefs and habits come from the most important and influential people in our life; our parents and teachers as we grew up and our friends and colleagues in adult life. Our beliefs and habits are a way of helping us interpret and understand the world, and whilst they can be positive, they often limit us too.

Have you ever said anything like the following to yourself?

You might not have said such things out loud, but found yourself thinking or feeling something similar without actually articulating it.

YOUR INNER VOICE

All these types of thoughts influence the way you live your life. You may have been lucky enough to receive positive influences that boosted your self-esteem, but for most of us it's been a mixture of positive and negative and guess which we tend to focus on? Just as performers remember the single critical comment over the many good ones, negative thoughts stick.

It's as if you have an inner voice talking to you. This self-talk or inner dialogue is like a continuous conversation going on in your mind in response to what you're thinking or doing.

So for example, when you were asked to think about the sort of life you would like, was there a part of you, a little voice inside, that made you reluctant to think big? Was there some self-talk going on about being afraid of dreaming too big in case you failed to achieve it? Or maybe your inner voice was telling you your desires weren't realistic for someone like you.

Most of the time we are not aware of the inner voice and self-talk going on in our minds all day every day. But it's there – taking its cue from our beliefs and habits whilst simultaneously reinforcing those beliefs and habits.

HOW TO IDENTIFY YOUR BELIEFS AND HABITS

A good way to identify the beliefs and habits you have is to take a look at your life now and compare it with what you want to change.

If you listen for the reaction within you about something you want to change, it can give you an idea of the sort of limitations your inner thoughts are placing on you.

You will do this for yourself in part 2, but for now here's a couple of examples to illustrate the point.

DO YOUR WANT MORE TIME?

Do you see your present life as a continual rush from one thing to the next, and want to change it to have more time for yourself? This by the way was pretty much how I saw my pre-*Changeability* life. If so what might this reveal about your beliefs?

You might say it means you have a lot to do. Yes, but if you were to dig underneath this first reaction, it could be you have an underlying belief you should be busy all the time.

This might be to justify the roles you have – at work, in the family, in the community; or to fulfil a work ethic. You may consider it morally good to utilize as much of your time as possible, or maybe deep down you feel you don't deserve time to yourself to do what you want. Perhaps you feel there's something intrinsically selfish about wanting your own personal time.

The reasons you feel like this could be many, including your role models, but the outcome is that without realizing it you've filled up all your time because of your underlying beliefs.

This is close to home for me as I found myself working 50 hours a week as a regional Learning Director for a Government organization. At the time serving as an elected Town Councillor, a School governor, a learning mentor, singing in two choirs, performing in amateur musical theatre, and of course doing the home, family and friends stuff. Some days I felt I hardly had time to go to the bathroom! Yet I can't deny you get a certain buzz from living like this, the pay off being the feeling you're getting things done and making the most of your time, which is of course the result of underlying beliefs.

You may be busy doing lots of worthy things but the bottom line is your beliefs and habits are getting in the way of change for you.

DO YOU WANT MORE MONEY?

If you're seeking a change in your financial situation it's worth exploring whether underlying fears based on your beliefs could be limiting your opportunities.

It might be a fear of failure or of success. Or you might be afraid that no one will like you, or worry about what your friends would think if you achieve great financial success.

If so, what does this type of thinking say about your beliefs around money and wealthy or successful people?

We'll come back to this example later as it is used to illustrate some of the techniques in part 2.

ARE YOUR STORIES SABOTAGING YOU?

These examples show how we can sabotage the very things we want because of the stories we tell ourselves, based on beliefs and habits built up over many years.

THE INVISIBLE INFLUENCE

The thing about habits is they are something you do or think over and over and that is when they become a habit.

By the time the habit is formed you don't specifically consider it but accept it as the way things are done, or as the truth, or as your way of seeing the world. Most of the time you don't think about habits at all but just get on with living life under their invisible influence, like a hidden script you're following.

However if you want to make changes in your life you need to become aware of them. Because although you believe them to be true, they're often limiting beliefs and habits that have become so ingrained you actually think you can't change or achieve things and in truth you end up being unable to. They become a self-fulfilling prophecy.

This is not in any way to trivialise important issues and beliefs, but rather to help us look at things in a different way. It's about finding a way to free yourself from the preconceptions and versions of your own truth that we all have.

They may have got in the way of you living the life you want until now, but the good news is firstly that acting in accordance with your beliefs and habits is perfectly natural and there are good reasons for it. Secondly, you can manage your mind to overcome this, turn it to your advantage and bring about the change you want.

To understand how this is possible let's look at how your marvellous brain works.

3. THE BRILLIANT YOU

"The mind, which sometimes presumes to believe that there is no such thing as a miracle, is itself a miracle." ~ M. Scott Peck

YOU ARE AMAZING!

Have you ever stopped and realized that you are in fact utterly amazing?

Well let me tell you, you are amazing – whatever you believe at present.

As you read this, your brain is processing a huge amount of information, including:

- Receiving the electrical impulses carried along your optic nerve from the light entering your eye's pupils.
- Interpreting these electrical impulses into what you 'see'.

- Translating the patterns you see into the words you're reading.
- Using the skill and habit of reading to make sense of these words.
- Comparing the meaning of the words with your views based on your experience.
- Perhaps considering whether you understand or believe what you're reading.
- Maybe following a line of thought imagining what it could mean for you.
- Possibly thinking of a memory sparked off by the words.
- And probably considering what you're having for your next meal.

At the same time your brain is thinking about all of this and more, it is also interpreting the sound waves entering your eardrums into what you're hearing; ensuring your body is balanced as you sit on your chair; keeping whatever you're reading this on at the right distance from your eyes and moving accordingly; plus the millions of functions it continually carries out to keep you alive. All going on without you really being aware of it.

A TALE OF TWO MINDS

Essentially, your brilliant mind is working on two levels, the conscious and subconscious (also known as the unconscious).

The analogy of an iceberg is often used to describe the relationship between these two levels. The tip of the iceberg represents the conscious mind, the part we are aware of like the tip of an iceberg seen above the water. The vast mass of ice underneath the sea is like the subconscious mind operating under the surface. And just as we only see the top 10% to 20% of the iceberg, about 15% of the brain's mass is taken up with conscious functions. However that's as far as the analogy goes, because the power and activity of the subconscious mind outweighs that of the conscious mind by a startling 1:1,000,000 (one to one million).

The relationship between the conscious and subconscious has been described as a flea riding on the back of an elephant, with the flea largely at the mercy of the elephant when it comes to the direction of travel.

We should not however underestimate the value of the conscious mind just because the subconscious is so much more powerful. They have different but complementary roles to play, and the trick is to get them playing together in harmony.

YOUR WONDERFUL CONSCIOUS BRAIN

Your conscious thinking brain is truly wonderful and what sets you apart from the rest of the animal kingdom. It gives you the ability to focus, learn and concentrate, to decide what you want to do, when and how to do it, and the will to put your decisions into action. It is responsible for your powers of reason, perception and intuition and enables you to make plans. It is where your incredible imagination in all its glory sits. It is truly magnificent.

However in spite of it's magnificence the conscious brain has limitations. It loses focus about every ten seconds and can only hold a limited amount of information at any one time, on average around seven 'chunks' of information (according to Dr George Miller, the pioneer of cognitive psychology).

Imagine having to think of everything you need to do to keep alive. It would be an impossible task given that most of us only retain about seven pieces of information at a time in the forefront of our thoughts. However it works because this is where the subconscious kicks in.

YOUR INCREDIBLE SUBCONSCIOUS BRAIN

Your subconscious is working all the time, 24 hours a day, a hidden force carrying out an unimaginable number of interactions. Regulating and maintaining your bodily functions; taking in oxygen and removing carbon dioxide, digesting and absorbing food to give you energy, keeping your heart beating, transporting nutrients and metabolic waste around your system, producing and regulating your hormones, controlling your body heat, seeking out and destroying unfriendly bacteria, ensuring the smooth movement of hundreds of muscles, and renewing three hundred million cells every minute. And that's just for starters!

Alongside the mammoth job of keeping your body working without you even thinking about it, your subconscious also oversees all the activities you've learned to do so well you do them without thinking. The automatic skills and habits like riding a bike, driving a car, reading, tying your laces, walking up and down stairs, or travelling a familiar route.

However, your subconscious brain is also continually engaged in another activity, which is particularly relevant to understanding why we act in certain ways and find it hard to make changes. This is the processing of information, and there are two important aspects to the way the subconscious part of our brain does this.

IS THAT A LIBRARY IN YOUR BRAIN?

We are all are subject to the constant bombardment of multiple stimuli from our environment. This information enters your brain through your senses and it's the job of the subconscious to decide how to react. It does this by comparing the new information with the existing data stored in your subconscious and formulating an appropriate response.

This storage facility is like a library in the brain. This brain library contains a record of all your experiences, skills, perceptions, values, beliefs, attitudes and habits.

So if you're suddenly alarmed by something, the subconscious takes previous similar situations, your beliefs about what you should do, and your habits in this type of circumstance, into account in making a decision on whether your response should be fight, flight or have a discussion.

This happens almost instantaneously. So much so that you're sometimes aware of your reaction before being conscious of what caused it.

This ability to instantly recognize a situation and determine your response to it is for the most part a very positive thing. It saves your conscious mind from having to continually think about the intricate details of your life and constantly make decisions about how to react. Most importantly it works to keep you safe by maintaining the status quo based on experience of what has worked so far (like hot things will burn you).

WHAT A BRAINY SEARCH ENGINE YOU HAVE

Have you ever bought something new and suddenly noticed how many other people have the same thing as you? Why didn't you notice it before? The answer lies in the second important aspect of subconscious activity and is key to understanding why we are a product of our beliefs and mindset.

You've just heard how the subconscious constantly takes in and deals with sensory data, most of which you are unaware of at a conscious level. You also know the conscious brain has a limited number of things it can focus on at one time. So your mind needs a filter mechanism to process the vast array of information it receives through its senses, and select the important things the conscious mind needs to be aware of from the millions of pieces of data available.

This role is carried out by a part of the brain called the reticular formation or reticular activating system (RAS). This network of nerve pathways at the base of your brain connects the spinal cord, cerebellum and cerebrum parts of the brain. It is responsible for the transition between being asleep and awake and for filtering all sensory inputs from your environment. This means it effectively acts as a filter to your world, constantly sorting everything you see, hear, taste, feel or smell and forwarding it to be processed by the appropriate part of the brain. As a result of this sifting process the RAS alerts your conscious mind to the information that's important to it.

So what criteria determines the relevant important information for the conscious brain to be made aware of, out of the millions of pieces of data coming in? This is where your brain turns into a search engine, because just as Google or Yahoo search for the string of words you enter into their search engine, your RAS will search out what you have programmed your brain to focus on. This could be the specific goals or ideas you want it to search for, but will also include evidence to support your belief systems, habits and ways of thinking based on your past experience.

That new item you're now seeing everywhere has always been there, but your filter system had not previously brought it to the forefront of your conscious mind because it wasn't part of your experience or thinking.

Now you're aware of this it's easy to see the evidence in your own life. When I was pregnant I suddenly started noticing lots of other pregnant women everywhere, and shops selling baby products or news items on children or pregnancy. When I was thinking of buying a BMW I was suddenly aware of all the same models on the road. All of these had always been there but weren't part of my conscious experience because they'd not been brought to the forefront of my conscious mind.

It's the same reason you wake up when your baby starts crying or your teenager comes creeping home late at night. Your brain is programmed to recognize your baby's cry or the sound of the creaking door and filter out the rest. So you wake up for these even though you've happily slept through the louder sounds that never made it to your conscious recognition, because your subconscious knew they didn't warrant waking up for in the middle of the night.

THAT'S ALL VERY INTERESTING BUT WHAT'S IT GOT TO DO WITH CHANGING YOUR LIFE?

Well quite a lot because it explains why it can be so difficult to make changes and not least because you have a subconscious that can hinder rather than assist your efforts.

BATTLE OF THE BRAINS

Have you ever decided to get fit or made a New Year's resolution to eat less? The first few days start well and then things seem to come along which take you off your path and before you know it you realize you've been doing nothing recently towards achieving your goal.

The clue to why this happens lies in the fact that the conscious mind may decide one thing but your underlying subconscious may believe something very different.

Take the example of the diet. Your conscious mind may feel it's really up for change – you've looked in the mirror and decided now is the time to kick-start that diet. Your subconscious, however, may take a different view based on its different beliefs, habits and emotional experiences. Remember that inner dialogue, in this case it's coming up with homespun pearls of wisdom such as 'I'm a naturally big person, 'it's hard to lose weight as you get older,' 'diets are so boring,' ' I have a slow metabolism', 'everyone deserves a treat' or even 'thin people are miserable'.

Unwittingly, the subconscious always wants to preserve the status quo. It fears change from our more primitive days when change meant danger and fight or flight. So even though the conscious mind has a desire for change, the subconscious has an even stronger desire to maintain things the way they are. And guess what, the subconscious tends to win.

WE LOVE LIVING IN COMFORT

Your conscious efforts are undermined by the good intentions of your subconscious to keep you safe by staying within familiar territory. This is of course territory in line with your beliefs about yourself, the world and your self-talk. When you stray outside of it you experience a sense of anxiety from being outside your comfort zone, or you feel fear, like the common fear of failure.

THE UNKNOWN UNKNOWNS

> *"There are known knowns; there are things we know we know. We also know there are known unknowns; that is to say, we know there are some things we do not know. But there are also unknown unknowns – the ones we don't know we don't know."* ~ Donald Rumsfeld

To compound this further we have seen how the unconscious brain filters out information outside of your experience and programming. However, this can mean you then don't see the opportunities right in front of your nose.

Your subconscious brain blocks them out as part of its gatekeeping role. It literally filters opportunity out of your horizons if it is:

- Information out of line with what is consciously placed in the forefront of your mind.
- Something that could upset the status quo.
- An experience outside of your belief system, habits and way of thinking about yourself
- Any combination of these and possibly all of them.

The upshot is the opportunity doesn't register with your conscious brain as something you need to know about, and therefore remains outside your experience. This is why it is an unknown 'unknown' – it hasn't been brought to your attention so you are unaware of the opportunity staring you in the face.

WHAT DOES THIS MEAN FOR CHANGING YOUR LIFE?

The logic of this is it's not your fault when you find it difficult to make changes in life or see goals through to completion. Your whole system is working to keep you safe and comfortable within the context of your current beliefs, habits and experience.

But this doesn't mean there's no role for your will or conscious thought to determine what you do, or for willpower to help you reach a target. You are not a helpless creature with a predetermined route through life based on your upbringing and biology without the ability to make changes.

Your conscious brain and will have crucially important roles to play, but we have seen that there is a lot more to it than that. It's not just a matter of deciding what you want and employing iron willpower to get it. Your internal dialogue can undermine you. The stories you tell yourself, your beliefs and habits, will result in reverting to type or not taking advantage of opportunities because you are blind to them.

WHAT'S THE IMPLICATION OF THIS?

It means that without the ability to change our underlying beliefs we are literally filtering out opportunity. If we don't believe we are ever capable of being rich, thin, happy, or whatever, then we fail to see those ever-present rich making, thin making, and ever-fizzing happy moments.

However the very thing holding you back is also the key to your transformation.

It is the common denominator behind your beliefs, self-talk and habits. It's your ways of thinking, and what lies behind the way you think – your thoughts.

So you need to change your thoughts and the way you think and this is where we are going next.

4. **YOUR BRILLIANT THOUGHTS**

"It's not what you have to 'do' that needs to change. It's first how you 'think' that needs to change. It's who you have to 'be' in order to 'do' what needs to be done. The good news is that it doesn't cost much money to change your thinking. In fact, it can be done for free." ~ Robert Kiyosaki

IT STARTED WITH A THOUGHT

Everything starts as a thought.

Every conscious action starts as a thought.

Every great idea (and not so great idea) starts as a thought.

From the small everyday activities we do so often they become habits, like cleaning our teeth, to more weighty decisions like what to have for lunch, to the most complex calculations, processes or activities we undertake, they all start with a thought.

All creative enterprise begins with a thought, an idea that precedes the creation of every novel, poem, painting and design.

Every great social and political movement commences with thinkers thinking thoughts prior to collecting and organising them into an ideology.

YOUR THOUGHTS ARE YOUR FUTURE

Spiritual teachers have long recognized the influence our thoughts have on our lives.

> *"All that we are is the result of what we have thought. The mind is everything. What we think, we become."* ~ Siddhartha Gautama (Buddha)

Our thoughts impact our emotions and feelings.

Our thoughts influence our bodies and physical and mental health. Even our biochemistry is affected by our thoughts according to genetics researcher Dr Bruce Lipton:

> *"Positive thoughts have a profound effect on behaviour and genes, and negative thoughts have an equally profound effect."*

Our thoughts attract other thoughts and affect our outlook, and like a self-fulfilling prophecy what we focus on is what we tend to get.

Our thoughts influence and create our future.

Our thoughts translate the present world into our perception of reality.

YOUR THOUGHTS MATTER

So your thoughts really are important. In the words of Dr Daniel G. Amen:

> *"Your thoughts matter. If you want to feel good, think good thoughts."*

The past two decades have seen enormous leaps forward in the way we understand the brain, allowing us to glimpse its magnificent workings and apply a scientific basis to what was previously the domain of spiritual and philosophical understanding and practice.

Modern imaging technology enables us to scan the brain as it thinks specific types of thoughts, and see the effect they have.

We can measure changes in different spheres of the brain over time owing to changes in thoughts and behaviour.

We can take the advances in neuroscience, sports science and psychology to influence how we bring about the change we want in any aspect of our lives.

We can use the scientific understanding to give us the confidence to think new thoughts, imagine new experiences, raise our expectations, tell new stories, set our goals higher and take life to the next level.

5. **TAKING THE CONTROLS**

"Every human has four endowments – self awareness, conscience, independent will and creative imagination. These give us the ultimate human freedom... The power to choose, to respond, to change." ~ Steven Covey

We've seen that change starts with a conscious thought, and also how it's often the subconscious that runs the show and can sabotage your best-laid plans for change. So although the conscious mind can determine what you want to do, your unconscious thoughts influence your doing it, based on your beliefs, habits and experience.

In other words, your conscious brain decides what action you want to take and your unconscious brain affects the way you carry out that action.

But both aspects are crucial for *Changeability* and getting the life you want. The trick is to get your conscious and unconscious thoughts working together and moving you in the same direction.

You therefore want to be aware of and find ways of managing your mind and changing your conscious and unconscious thoughts.

THINK ABOUT WHAT YOU THINK ABOUT

When things don't go the way we think they should or want them to, we feel upset, disappointed or hard done by and sometimes think life isn't fair or shouldn't be like this. Mostly it's a fleeting thought we dismiss as childish or unrealistic before moving on to deal with the situation, but sometimes we're left with a sense of injustice.

We feel that life or the world is out to get us, or ask why bad things always seem to happen to us. We look for someone or something to blame (like our parents, God, the boss) for the things we don't like about our life. We may not actually come right out and say these things but have a vague unarticulated awareness lurking in our thoughts. We know it's not logical but it doesn't stop us.

If any of this rings true (and we probably all feel like this sometimes) the problem is it places us in the role of victim where we're are being 'done to'. And when you see yourself as a victim you relinquish power and control over to someone or something else.

So although inner thoughts of this kind are common, they are totally unhelpful for getting the changes you want in life. Remembering also you tend to attract the things you focus on, and your inner dialogue can limit your opportunities, it's well worth being aware of and working to change the way you react.

This starts with changing the way you think, which means choosing thoughts that will get you what you want.

A FABULOUS REALIZATION

One of the most amazing realizations of all is that we can influence the thoughts we think!

Think about what this means for a minute.

If our thoughts have such a huge impact on how we live, and we can choose them – then surely we can start to choose how we live, choose how we respond, choose how we talk to ourselves, choose to change and choose our future.

You can use the very thing that has been holding you back to move you forward. And in doing so take the most liberating step of all – you take control.

Taking control means taking responsibility for your life – not in a boring, dull or dutiful way but in a joyful exciting and freeing way.

It doesn't mean unpleasant or horrible things will never happen to you, or you'll never experience grief or sadness, these are part of the experience of being alive. But it does mean you recognize you have some power over how you react. This includes the manner in which you choose to accept circumstances totally beyond your influence.

This notion of choice is a crucial point. Your conscious thoughts are one thing you have control over. You are not a helpless being tossed about by life. You are an intelligent being with the power to determine your thoughts and actions and make the changes you need to get the life you want.

THAT AHA MOMENT

For everyone who is serious about developing their *Changeability* and making positive change in their life there comes a point where this notion of choice and taking charge becomes absolutely real to you. A moment when it clicks into place and you totally get the concept.

Here are a couple of 'aha' moments to give you a flavour of what I mean.

One day a few years ago I was out walking my dog along the riverbank. But instead of admiring the beautiful view, I was totally focussed on stewing over something happening at work. Following a restructure, I and the other Learning Directors had been awarded a lower pay grade than our employer facing colleagues. As I walked along thinking (not for the first time) about how unjust it was and no way reflected the value of our work, I knew I didn't like the way thinking about this made me feel. Frustration, resentment and anger are not pretty emotions. Then it hit me – a moment of clear realization about how we can choose to react to situations.

Having read many personal development books and undertaken coaching and mentoring courses to develop myself and others, I knew the theory and understood the concept. But in that moment of clarity as I walked along thinking about this concept and the amazing notion that we can choose how we react, it came to me that if this is really so then I could put the theory into practice. Why not make the choice right now to do something about this situation I was so unhappy about, but had considered totally outside my control?

I realized in that instant that I was responsible for the resentment I felt about this perceived injustice being 'done to me', and had cast myself in the role of victim. I knew that although I wasn't responsible for the situation, I was responsible for my reaction to it.

So acknowledging that I may or may not be able to change the eventual outcome but could choose my response, I decided to take a course of well considered action. Starting with examining the inner dialogue that potentially held me back, thoughts like will people think I'm greedy and how will I feel if they say I'm not worth it, I took the bull by the horns. Knowing that whatever the eventual outcome, I had taken control and done my best to see it through. More on what I actually did later, but for now I'm happy to say it resulted in the most satisfactory outcome of an extra £10,000 salary per annum.

This is how Julian, my husband and partner at BrilliantLivingHQ.com, described what he called his *eureka* moment which, as is so often the case, occurred whilst in the shower (too much information maybe).

> *"Twelve months earlier had been traumatic. I'd been sitting at a work conference when news of the change of government seemed to permeate the room. We all knew the significance of this moment and the conference couldn't quite hold its head up after that. The project I and others had been working on had been a great 5 years but everyone in that room knew the new government meant austerity measures, and let's face it as an initiative of the now 'previous' government we were likely candidates for the inevitable cuts that were coming. That would mean*

one thing – redundancy. There was a palpable air of quiet panic in the room.

Fast forward a year and the fears were becoming a reality for people. Kathryn and I talked of how with everyone facing austerity measures, we needed solutions to help people take control and live the life they want.

We'd been kicking around the problems of when you get stuck wanting to change but can't quite get going or get out of where you are. One day in the shower I found myself pondering problems like negative self-belief, lack of direction or knowing what you want, of being in the wrong frame of mind; and how all of these needed to be overcome to move forward and achieve your goals. I thought to myself that these problems were like a vicious circle and then the image of a coin came to mind. In an instant I knew that the very things that trapped us and prevented us living the life we want were the limiting beliefs, self-talk and negative thoughts in our mind. And if we could get the mind to use these but in a positive way, the flip side of the coin so to speak, we could change our negatives into positives and change our lives.

So that's what I did for myself. I chose to positively deal with the uncertainly and threat of impending redundancy, and together with Kathryn went on to create Brilliant Living HQ .com to help others use their minds to live their best lives." ~ Julian Illman

In that aha moment Julian realized that if his thoughts were influencing his actions in a negative way, they could also be used to have a positive impact.

SELF-EFFICACY

We went on to live out this notion of taking charge of our lives in bigger and bolder ways to get the change we wanted. Such realizations are key to *Changeability.*

They demonstrate what is known in psychology as self-efficacy. Self-efficacy is a hugely important concept for *Changeability.* It means having belief in your ability to influence events affecting you.

> *"When you have self-efficacy, it means the source and centre of control in your life is internal, not external. Misfortunes and other external influences cannot completely throw you, because you see yourself as being at the 'cause' rather than at the 'effect' of circumstances. You cannot always 'fix' the circumstance or solve the external problem, but you can always shift how you perceive it."* ~ George Pratt Ph.D. and Peter Lambrou, Ph.D.

This is how we came to view the end of the university project Julian managed, as a massive opportunity rather than a disaster. This is how I came to walk away from the secure option of a well-paid career.

We wanted more from our lives and we wanted it now, not when we retired at some future point in time. We believed we had the power to exercise self-efficacy and take the controls to create the life we wanted to live. We had *Changeability* and so do you.

MORE THAN POSITIVE THINKING

There's more to this than positive thinking, important though that is.

This is not just about positive thinking in a whimsical superficial way. It doesn't mean that by thinking happy thoughts you will get everything you want.

It is about changing the way you think and feel about yourself and your life at every level, consciously and unconsciously, and using the changed you to take action to get the life you want.

It's like reprogramming the computer that is your brain. Replacing the software with new code that tells another story and opens you up to new opportunities.

Placing yourself in the driver seat, taking charge of the direction you are going, is at the heart of all change. It is the secret to getting a better life. It is also the most positive, invigorating, energising, empowering, liberating leap into the future you can take.

The wonderful news is that there are techniques and tools to propel you towards the life you want. So let's go to the action of part two, where you get to change and create the life you want.

> *"The measure of intelligence is the ability to change."* ~
> Albert Einstein

part 2

THE CHANGEABILITY PROGRAMME

10 STEPS FOR CHANGE

6. **THE CHANGEABILITY PROGRAMME**

"If you don't like how things are, change it! You're not a tree." ~ Jim Rohn

This is where change starts as you take the 10 *Changeability* steps and put them into action.

Each step is a technique, with explanation and guided actions to take to start changing what you want to change.

The programme is designed to be sequential with each step building on the previous one, so I suggest you initially go through each step in the order set out. However once you've completed it and got to grips with the techniques, they can all be used individually according to your needs and preference.

First a couple of practical points.

THE CHANGEABILITY ACTION WORKSHEETS

As mentioned earlier, you can download the free Action Worksheets from http://www.BrilliantLivingHQ.com/changeabilityws. These bring together the actions and tools of Part 2 in a Word format for your convenience so you can complete them on your computer if you wish. You can also copy and paste your outcomes from one step into the next, which will make sense as you do the techniques that progressively build on one another. Alternatively you can print them out and write down your answers. You don't have to use the worksheets to get value from the rest of this book but they are a practical convenient way to encourage yourself to take action.

At the end of this book there's a summary chapter that includes a table of all the techniques and actions. This gives you an overview of everything in one place and how they fit together, so you don't have to remember it all as you go through each step. And don't forget the quick start actions at the end of each step – if you do nothing else – do these!

Let's get started with Step 1.

7. **STEP 1. VISION SETTING**

"Would you tell me, please, which way I ought to go from here?"
"That depends a good deal on where you want to get to," said the Cat.
"I don't much care where," said Alice.
"Then it doesn't matter which way you go," said the Cat
"So long as I get SOMEWHERE," Alice added as an explanation.
"Oh, you're sure to do that," said the Cat, "if you only walk long enough." ~ Lewis Carroll

The first step on the route to your changed life is to create the vision of what that changed life will look like, which we'll call your brilliant life.

If you don't have an end game in sight, how will you know what you're aiming for? If you have nothing to aim for there is every chance you will wander aimlessly through life, getting tossed about like a rudderless boat on the sea and ending up wherever the current takes you.

This is absolutely fine if it's how you want to live, but the fact you've made it this far into the book shows it doesn't apply to you.

You want change and this is where you decide what your changed life will look like.

> "Possibly the trickiest part of getting what you want in life is just figuring out what you really want! And yet it is certainly the most important part of all." ~ Shakti Gawain

In this step you're creating the destination that the rest of the techniques will drive you towards, so it's worth spending some time on it.

You're going to think about how you want your life to be and your answers will form the basis of your goals. Now you may already know exactly what you want to change and what your changed life will look like. If so you don't need Action 1A to help you get clear on this, but may still find it interesting and useful.

You may however find it more difficult to pin down your goals than you'd expect. If so, don't worry; this is common and not surprising given that most of us spend more time and effort planning our next holiday than our life.

We're busy getting on with day-to-day living and rarely stop and think 'What do I want out of my life – really want?' So when we do, it can make us feel uneasy, even irritated at our inability to articulate what we want our lives to look like.

If this is the case don't be hard on yourself, just accept that your underlying beliefs and mechanisms for maintaining the status quo are making you feel uncomfortable. We will look at ways of making them work for you rather than against you in the following steps, but for now just follow the actions for step one – setting your vision and goals.

ACTION 1A: STARTING OUT

- To help focus your vision and goal setting, take a look at the list below of different aspects of life and some ideas about what they can include. Give yourself a score out of 10 for how satisfied you are with each category (10 = totally satisfied, 0 = totally unsatisfied).

SATISFACTION WITH LIFE – STARTER FOR 10

- **Career and work** – dream job, skills, own business, promotion, fulfilment.
- **Money** – extra income, debt-free, financial freedom.
- **Health and body** – fitness, wellness, weight, appearance, energy.
- **Relationships** – partner, family, friends, colleagues, pets.
- **Lifestyle and leisure** – interests, experiences, travel, hobbies, holidays.
- **Community** – home and abroad, charity, religion, politics, volunteering, contribution.
- **Time** – self, family and friends, work-life balance.
- **Possessions** – house, car, technology, fashion, interests.

- **Personal development and self-expression** – investment, creativity, clear vision, spirituality.
- **Values, behaviours and characteristics** – fun, enthusiasm, excitement, security, integrity, truth.

For example, in the first category, career and work, you might consider where you are in relation to your dream job or the promotion you want. Whether you have the right skills for the career you want, or how near you are to your ideal of setting up your business. Score it out of 10.

You can visually capture your scores on a table from http://www.brilliantlivinghq.com/changeabilityws or make your own version. You will end up with something like this.

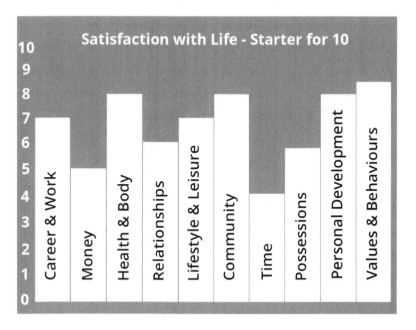

You may think you've just written down a few numbers or filled in a few boxes, but think again because you've achieved the following:

- You have created a starting point or baseline.
- You can see at a glance the areas of life furthest from what you would like them to be. This will help you prioritise the parts you want to focus on changing.
- You have covered some key areas of life and can choose to rectify imbalances between them when you set your goals.
- You have created a useful tool for evaluating your progress. You can repeat this process in 3, 6, 12 months to see how your scores change.

When I started out with this step it showed I wanted to focus on the areas of time, career and work, lifestyle, personal development and values and behaviours. These things then informed my vision and goals and were all interlinked for me. So my vision came to include a lifestyle where I had freedom over my time and talents, could be creative and use my skills and experience to help others and myself, and to do it with fun excitement and enthusiasm.

The exciting moment has arrived when you decide what your brilliant post-change life will look like. (And your opportunity to use the ideas you came up with earlier about your vision.)

ACTION 1B: A VISION OF SUCCESS

To set effective goals you need to first be clear about the vision of what your want to achieve. In other words, you need to define what your changed life looks like so you get rid of uncertainty and see the path to take.

- Imagine you are living the life you want to live. This is life after you've changed what you want to change. Imagine every aspect of your brilliant life. In other words what does success look like to you?
- Spend a few minutes writing down your vision for your brilliant life. Use your scores from 1A to think about the different areas of life you'd like to include and don't worry about making it perfect. You might like to write it out in a paragraph, like a story, for example:

  'In my brilliant life... *I live in a cottage near the sea with my wonderful partner, two lovely children and an adorable black curly haired dog. I have a fantastically successful and fulfilling career as a ... and am highly respected as a leader in my field. I earn ... per year ... I love being a parent and am doing a great job bringing up our happy children ... I enjoy all the fun and excitement of family life ... I have a loving relationship ... etc.'*

Of course your story will look very different. You might be jetting round the world working in exotic places, you might be surrounded by the fruits of your creative pursuits, you might be a popular musician or winning sportsperson, you might be working out in the gym or running along the beach looking fit and healthy, or you might be a super successful business person.

Like David, who dreamt of leaving his job to become an artist. But David's vision wasn't just for himself but to set up a whole community of mosaic artists and volunteers to create art for the public realm and make the streets of London even more beautiful. Today Southbank Mosaics is a thriving social enterprise with over

250 mosaic installations around London created by top mosaic artists and hundreds of volunteers, with many more exciting projects to come.

Whatever your story, it's a vision for your brilliant life. I hope it's something that gives you a tingle of excitement or leaves you grinning as you imagine your amazing future.

ACTION 1C: DEFINING YOUR DESIRES – STATING YOUR INTENTIONS

The next thing is to turn your vision and desires into your goals and intentions. This involves taking the essence of your vision, breaking it down into themes or areas (goals can be used in any area of your life and business,) and specifying the outcomes.

There are certain ways of setting goals and intentions that make them more effective. We're going to look at these now, and to make it easy to remember they all begin with P (sort of). You'll want to keep these in mind as you define your desires and set your intentions. They will boost the power generated by clearly articulating what you are going to achieve.

THE 5 'P'S OF CHANGEABILITY GOALS

1. Personal

First make sure all your goals are yours. That's to say they are applicable and important to you as an individual. Sometimes you think you want something but in truth you're doing it for someone else, a significant other such as a parent, loved one, or even your religion. Or it's something that you think you should want or would be good for you, even though deep down it's not what you really want or are interested in.

However well meaning you or others might be, you will not be committed to goals that don't grab you. This is not about doing what you think you should do, nor a laborious process to be worked through, but a stimulating inspiring exploration of your future, so own your goals for yourself. For this reason each of your goals will start with 'I'.

2. Present

Frame goals and intentions in the present tense. That is, compose them as if they are happening here and now, not at some future time. State your goals from the perspective of actively achieving them now. So e.g. starting with *'My goals are ...'* say 'I am financially secure' rather than 'I will be financially secure in five years'.

It might seem a strange way to put it but it is more powerful to state how your changed life looks when it becomes reality, rather than how it looks from where you are standing now.

This is important because it sends a strong clear signal to your mind that this is the reality it needs to be working to create right now, not filing it away as something that doesn't need to concern you for five years. This will be reinforced by the other techniques.

3. Positive

Keep the language positive. This means phrasing your statements in the positive not the negative. For example, if you want to lose weight, say 'I am slim' or 'I am a size 10' rather than 'I'm no longer overweight'.

You are saying what you want rather than what you don't want. Once again this sends a clear command to your brain. It is more effective to state the intended result rather than internally interpreting what something you don't want looks like.

It's difficult to think about and measure a negative or something that's not there. A positive is more measurable and more likely to lead you to actions that focus on your preferred outcome. The more specific you can be about clarifying what that outcome looks like the better.

4. Purpose

Being clear on the reasons why you are doing what you are doing, is crucial to creating goals that inspire you. The purpose behind your goals is the 'why' that will be your motivation.

For example, many people create a goal around finance. Indeed financial security is used as the example throughout this programme. However, while the goal is about wealth, the purpose behind it is not to get money for it's own sake, but as the means to get the things and experiences in life you desire. Like freedom, more time with family and friends, a sense of security for your family's future, experiences like travel or having your own boat or horse, or the ability to help others. These are the purpose behind the desire for money.

Make sure that whatever lies behind you wanting to attain your goals is important enough to you to ignite and sustain your commitment to accomplishing them.

It might be your husband, wife, children, family, friends, health, happiness, excitement, security, time with loved ones, recognition, reward, longevity, happiness, accomplishment, excitement, contentment, enjoyment, satisfaction, freedom, fulfilment, validation, sense of pride, control, love, safety, and so the list goes on – but whatever it is – make it big, because the bigger your 'why' the easier the going will be.

> *"Humans work best when they have a sense of purpose. It doesn't seem to matter what it is, as long as there is one! Without a sense of purpose the Human lacks direction and meaning to life."* ~ Dr Steve Peters

5. Pen or Print

It's writing really, but I wanted another 'P' to finish off the list! Last but not least it's critical to write down your goals. In writing down your goals you define and declare your intentions. Remember the reticular activating system from earlier, well when you write down your defined precise goals you give your brain something new to look for. It's like giving your mind a new set of eyes to see with, or co-ordinates on your mental satellite navigation system.

What you are doing here is setting new parameters for your experience. You are clearly stating your new intention, and in doing so start to shift your focus and energy onto the actions and opportunities that coincide with getting you on track towards your vision.

CRAFTING YOUR GOALS

It's time to create your goals and record your intentions.

- Using your vision of brilliant living from 1B as a guide for the themes you want to include, write out up to 5 statements that sum up your goals. Remember to create them in line with the 5 Ps, so they are personal, in the present tense, use positive language, have a clear underlying purpose and are written down.

  For example: *I have ... financial freedom*

If you want to focus on changing one thing in your life for the time being (like losing weight or having more time), then write goals around that area of your life. It can be a good strategy to focus on one change at a time, even though in practice you may find yourself changing more than one aspect of your life. E.g. if you want to be slimmer you might increase your exercise which makes you fitter and healthier as well. If you concentrate on one change now, you can always revisit the vision to take a broader approach in the future.

As you formulate your intentions it's helpful to differentiate between the ends and the means. You want to focus on the ends. This is similar to being clear about your purpose but can be a useful distinction to make.

To go back to the finance example, you may think straight off you want a goal of making a million pounds, but actually the million pounds is the means to get you to the end you want, which is financial freedom or increased status or whatever you think having that money will bring you.

Keeping this in mind as you set your goals will help to focus you on what you really want, rather than the means to get it (which we come to later). This is why it's important to start with your end vision and reverse engineer it, working backwards to find out what your goals are.

You can tweak or change your goals at any time, so take it seriously but don't agonise over it. It is better to get something down than to take so long you lose impetus and put it off until you can get it perfect. The important thing is you do it!

QUICK START GOALS

A simple quick way to find your goals is take whatever you want to change and write down three phrases to describe what your life looks like after you've changed it.

(For example, if you want to change your weight you might describe your changed life as 'I weigh 140lbs. I am a size 10. I enjoy buying new clothes'.)

You now have a list of statements that clearly state what you want your life to look like. These are your goals.

Congratulations on taking the first big practical *Changeability* step – you have created the goals and set the intentions for where you're headed.

8. **STEP 2. TAKING STOCK**

"Sometimes we adopt certain beliefs when we're children and use them automatically when we become adults, without ever checking them out against reality. This brings to mind the story of the woman who always cut off the end of the turkey when she put it in the oven. Her daughter asked her why, and her mother responded, 'I don't know. My mother always did it.' Then she went and asked her mother, who said, 'I don't know. My mother always did it.' The she went and asked her grandmother, who said, 'The oven wasn't big enough.'" ~ Charlotte Davis Kasl

Be very aware – self-aware!

You've set down your vision and intentions for how your changed life looks, and in doing so have created your direction of travel and destination goals.

Now it's time to take stock, and that means taking a look at where you're starting out from. This is because you're going to identify the underlying beliefs and thought habits that have the potential to sabotage your *Changeability* and block your route to brilliant living. These are the unhelpful self-beliefs that limit growth and opportunity, and get in your way of making changes you want to make, becoming the person you want to be and living a life you love.

These are your *limiting beliefs* that need to be recognized and dealt with. The best way to do this is to begin by looking at your life now; this is your starting point.

If you're serious about moving forward, it's important to go through this stage in order to be aware of what's holding you back from making the changes you want.

Don't be tempted to skip this step. Go with it and be fascinated.

ACTION 2A: BELIEFS INVENTORY

- Take each of the goals you created in 1C in turn and write a few words to sum up how your life looks now at this starting point in relation to the goal. (There's an example at the end of this section.)

- Now sit quietly and read the goal in your head and out loud. As you do this be aware of the reaction within you as you declare your intention by stating your goal. This is about listening to your inner voice, or having a conversation with yourself as you think around the subject matter (health, weight, wealth, work, relationships or whatever it is).

- Note down whatever comes into your mind. It may be one thought or several, it doesn't matter – just write them down. These are your self-beliefs. You are most interested in those with the potential to limit you in some way, the limiting beliefs that don't support the changes you want.

Keep in mind you're trying to get inside your thoughts. It's not about what you think you should believe, or say you believe about yourself or others, but what your innermost thoughts are actually telling you. It's about what the little voice inside you is really saying – even if it's not what you want to hear.

Be absolutely honest with yourself, otherwise there is little point in doing it. You don't need to share this with anyone, so write whatever rings true for you.

Here's an example to illustrate the technique. The example of financial freedom is used throughout the book to enable us to follow a goal through the course of the techniques. It doesn't mean I think money is the key to happiness, but it is important and something that many people want to make changes around.

BELIEFS INVENTORY		
Starting point	**Limiting beliefs**	**Vision and goals**
Credit card debt *Overdraft / Bank loan* *Never quite enough money at the end of every month*	*People like me don't get wealthy* *There's never enough to go round* *Rich people are basically selfish and greedy* *I'll never have enough money* *If I get more someone else gets less* *I don't deserve great wealth* *My wealth is at someone else's expense* *I'll never earn that sort of money* *I have to struggle to get what I want*	*I have financial freedom*

You may find further insights come to you in the next few days, if so add them. It's also helpful to note down phrases you find yourself saying or thinking as you go about your day that illustrate or hint at your self-beliefs e.g. I'm unlucky; why am I always ill; I'm too old for that?

Most people would think that at age 76 Harriet Thompson was too old to take up marathon running. Yet pushing aside the limiting beliefs many of us have about age, Harriet recently completed her 15th marathon at the age of 91 and set a new U.S. record. And only one month after undergoing radiotherapy treatment for cancer. Harriet's words of wisdom for those who don't think age is just a number; "*You're never too old to do it. Never think you're too old because I'm proof that you're not.*"

QUICK START BELIEFS STOCKTAKE

Say your goal out loud and immediately write down the first five things that come into your head.

You'll find your limiting beliefs lurking in amongst what you've written!

9. STEP 3.

CLEARING THE

GROUND

"The secret of change is to focus all of your energy, not on fighting the old, but on building the new." ~ Socrates

Although it might make uncomfortable reading, the process of identifying and writing your list of limiting thoughts and beliefs can be an enlightening experience. You are looking at the very beliefs and attitudes that block the way to achieving what you want.

These are the beliefs and ways of thinking we accept as truth because they are in line with our view of the world. We constantly reinforce this 'truth' through continually finding evidence to back up this view.

Let's return to the example goal of financial freedom. If your view of the world is that rich people are basically selfish and greedy, you won't have to look far to find evidence to support this version of your truth. However such thinking ignores those who use their wealth to improve their communities and the lives of others.

More importantly this thinking has a damaging effect on you achieving your goal of financial freedom (in this example, but applies to any goal). You create an inner conflict when you tell yourself you want more wealth but have negative connotations about wealthy people.

In addition, your brain's filtering system will not alert your consciousness to those wealth-creating opportunities out of line with your present beliefs. Those very opportunities which would change your present situation.

So it is important to recognize these negative self-limiting beliefs, see them for what they are, and let them go. You've identified these beliefs in Step 2, and now in Step 3 you'll examine them and clear them out.

ACTION 3A: EXPLORING YOUR LIMITING BELIEFS

Action 3A is about exploring your limiting beliefs so you get to see them for what they really are and can begin to dissipate their power.

- Take each limiting belief from Action 2A and ask yourself the following questions about it noting down a few words to sum up your response.

  - Am I experiencing an emotional reaction to this belief e.g. fear, guilt, hurt, anger, sadness, or a memory of a past negative event?

- Do I really believe and know for definite that this belief is actually a true statement or likely outcome?
- If I don't know that this statement is actually true, could I be mistaken and if so what would it mean for the belief?
- Am I generalising e.g. people like me / I never / always / can't?
- Am I labelling myself by assigning an all-embracing behaviour or characteristic to me e.g. I'm stupid / a failure?
- Does this belief support me in achieving my goal and if not how might it be changed to help rather than hinder me?

As you do this activity, be honest but gentle on yourself. Simply accept without judgement that you held this belief and acknowledge you want to move on.

Here is an example:

EXPLORING MY LIMITING BELIEFS CHECKLIST

Questions to ask about each belief:

1. Am I experiencing an emotional reaction or negative memory?

2. Do I really believe it and know it is true? What does it mean to my belief if I could be mistaken?

3. Am I generalising?

4. Am I labelling myself?

5. Does this belief support me achieving my goal?

Limiting beliefs	What I notice
People like me don't get wealthy	*Use questions 1-5 above as a guide* *1. Feel insignificant; who do I think I am. Remember when I didn't feel good enough, intimidated, not part of the right circle.* *2. No, I don't actually know it's true as although I think it unlikely, people like me do sometimes get wealthy. This means I could be mistaken in my belief, which means that people like me could get wealthy, and therefore I could.*

	3. Yes I'm generalising about 'people like me' whatever that might mean and about their ability to get wealthy.
	4. Yes I'm labelling myself as part of a particular group, with certain group characteristics possibly undeserving or of a certain class or education level.
	5. No, this belief does not support me achieving my goal of financial freedom.

When you find yourself thinking in ways that generalise your beliefs about your behaviour, it's worth remembering there will be times where the generalisation does not hold true. Just because something might often be the case (according to your beliefs) it doesn't mean it always is. And as it isn't always true then each example should be taken on it's own merits. Generalisation is therefore an unhelpful way of thinking.

It's also unhelpful to label yourself as inhabiting or exhibiting certain behaviours or characteristics. Whilst such thinking relieves you of responsibility e.g. I can't do that because I'm too stupid, it also takes away your power to act.

This is the opposite of what you want, and is untrue as no one totally embodies one characteristic such as stupidity. We might do things some describe as stupid but that is their subjective view and doesn't mean our whole being is defined by stupidity. Any all-embracing negative definitions and labels are therefore factually inaccurate and totally unhelpful.

You now have a list of beliefs that have held you back from

achieving change. You have looked at each belief and seen it for what it is, not an immovable truth but an unhelpful, untruthful, limiting set of thoughts that block progress to the life you want.

Well done on getting to this point. You have managed to do what most people never do – look at where they are now, identify negative limiting beliefs and see them for what they are.

You are exercising self-efficacy and taking charge of your direction. Now comes the clearing of these negative limiting beliefs, where you release them from your mind through the power of your conscious thought and a physical symbolic action.

ACTION 3B: RELEASING YOUR LIMITING BELIEFS THROUGH MENTAL SYMBOLISM

- Take a blank piece of paper and write out your list of limiting beliefs from 2A

- Sit down and relax. You're going to imagine a symbolic releasing of these beliefs so read through this next action before doing it, as ideally you want to have your eyes closed as you see it in your mind's eye. (You might need to take a quick peek if you can't remember your limiting beliefs.)

- Imagine you are standing in front of a casket or chest, like a treasure chest, only it's not treasure that's going into this chest. Now imagine taking each of the limiting beliefs on your list (and any associated negative emotions and painful memories) and placing them one by one into the casket. Once they are all in there bang the lid shut on them and close the latches tight. Now in your mind's eye see the casket being carried onto a sailing boat. Now watch as the boat casts off and is carried on the tide out to sea, until it disappears over the horizon and out of sight along with all your negative limiting beliefs.

You can achieve the same effect by imagining the casket being placed into the basket of a hot air balloon, and watching it float off up into the sky until it drifts out of sight over the horizon or into space.

Or you can devise your own version of a releasing scene by coming up with a vessel or container to place your limiting beliefs in and a vehicle or mechanism for transporting them away from you and out of sight.

ACTION 3C: RELEASING YOUR LIMITING BELIEFS THROUGH PHYSICAL SYMBOLISM

- Next take the piece of paper with your list of limiting beliefs and tear it into pieces.

- Throw the pieces away, or for best effect take the torn pieces of paper outside and burn them, consciously focusing on the release of your negative beliefs as you see the smoke rise and the paper disappear.

This is a deceptively simple process. Rather surprisingly it seems the actual process of identifying and acknowledging the limiting beliefs and associated emotions, followed by acceptance of their untrue nature and the need to let them go, is enough to release them, augmented with the symbolic clearing techniques.

You may therefore only need to do this once, but the method can be repeated for hard-core negative self-beliefs that linger or emerge over time.

This process can bring a sense of closure to the memories and emotions that underlie the habitual thinking that led to the constrictive limiting belief. (As with all techniques in this programme, if you have experienced trauma or abuse you may wish to seek the services of a professional therapist.)

QUICK START RELEASE

In your mind's eye imagine each of your limiting beliefs floating past you inside a thought bubble. Reach out and burst each one as you realize it's not true, and watch them dissolve into thin air.

Having released the self-defeating negative beliefs, the way is clear to create the new, inspiring, enabling beliefs to underpin your new worldview and empower you to achieve the life you want.

10. STEP 4. POSITIVE AFFIRMATIONS

CREATING EMPOWERING SELF-BELIEFS

"Did your phone just play "You Are My Sunshine'?" he asked. "Uh-huh. It's a personalized ring tone. It's affirming." He laughed, until the dignified raising of her eyebrows told him she was serious. "Affirmations are good for your self-esteem," she told him. "Every time my phone tells me I'm its sunshine, it makes me feel good." ~ Abbey Gaines

Wow – you have come a long way in just three steps. This has been the crucial legwork that increases the efficacy of this next technique.

So far you have looked at what you want to change in your life (your starting point) and what your changed life will look like (your goals). You have identified the underlying assumptions, attitudes and beliefs keeping you where you are now and limiting the opportunities available to you (your limiting beliefs). Having searched these you have discovered they are unhelpful, untruthful beliefs, which you released from your mind thereby clearing the way to install empowering positive beliefs.

Remember why it's important to create these positive thought patterns and beliefs.

Without the ability to change our underlying beliefs we are literally filtering out opportunities to help us change our lives. If we don't believe we are capable of the change we want, we fail to see the possibilities around us because our subconscious is not bringing them to the front of our consciousness.

Our thoughts are the key. The way we think influences the way we feel and the way we feel influences the way we act, the way we act determines the outcomes we get – how we live our lives and achieve our goals or not. The bottom line is that we therefore need to change our thoughts to change our behaviour. (This by the way is the basic idea underpinning cognitive therapy.)

Now starts the thrilling part where you begin to create your new story. Get set to make and install new beliefs to bring the change you want and the success you deserve.

AFFIRM YOURSELF

You do this through producing and absorbing powerful statements that declare and assert new positive self-beliefs that support your goals, aspirations and intentions.

You replace your old negative inner commentary with sparkling new programming featuring positive empowering dialogue based on your new beliefs and assumptions.

You *affirm* or *make firm* your new attitudes, views and beliefs. Hence this type of statement is often called an *affirmation.*

Although a slightly unusual and old-fashioned word in everyday conversation, affirmation is a particularly useful one in this context. Affirmation conveys both the notion of confirming or verifying something that is already so. It is *making firm* or *real* what you are thinking about, along with connotations of support and encouragement. This is all helpful in terms of making it real.

In other words you are affirming that your new empowering beliefs already exist and in doing so help to bring about the reality.

POSITIVE AND PRESENT

For this reason it's important to use the present tense when creating your affirmations, rather than the future, which is always ahead of you as far as your subconscious is concerned. You assume they are in place now e.g. 'I have enough money now' or 'I have all the money I need' rather than 'I will have enough money'.

Affirmations are empowering statements of what you want, rather than what you don't want, so should be positive in tone e.g. 'I have everything I need' rather than 'I am no longer in debt'. Your brain picks up the key words, so make them positive.

ACTION 4A: CREATING YOUR PERSONAL AFFIRMATIONS

- Take each negative limiting belief (from 2A) and change it into a positive empowering belief statement that will support you achieving your goals. You essentially flip the limiting belief around to create your affirmation. (There's an example below.)

- Write out your affirmation statements remembering to keep them positive and in the present tense. Ensure they are relevant to you, as these are the new personal beliefs that will sustain you in getting the change you want.

What you are doing here is affirming your new way of thinking. It's best to think of it in terms of where you are now moving to, rather than focusing on or being critical of your past or where you are now. Simply recognize how your thoughts to date have not helped you get what you want and now it's your time and opportunity to change. For this reason it's helpful to add an affirmation such as 'I love and fully accept myself' at the beginning of your list. It sets a good tone.

As you write your affirmations think of them as beliefs that expand and enhance your experience of life and open up opportunity, as opposed to contracting beliefs that constrict, stifle and limit your experience and close down opportunity.

Here is an example of affirmations based on the finance goal we've been using:

CREATING EMPOWERING BELIEFS		
Limiting beliefs	**Empowering beliefs: Affirmations**	**Vision & goals**
People like me don't get wealthy	*I love and fully accept myself*	*I have financial freedom*
Rich people are selfish and greedy	*I am the sort of person that has great wealth*	
I'll never have enough money	*The wealthier I am, the more I have to share*	
If I get more someone else gets less	*I always have all the money I need now*	
I don't deserve great wealth	*I live in an abundant world* *I totally deserve great wealth and success now*	
My wealth is at someone else's expense	*There is plenty to go round for me and everyone*	
I'll never earn that sort of money	*Exciting wealth creating opportunities are opening up for me today*	
I have to struggle to get what I want	*Money is flowing to me* *Making money comes easily to me*	

Financial guru Suze Orman was working as a waitress for ten years, had little money and felt unworthy to work on Wall Street, until she changed her thinking. She went on to become an Emmy Award winning TV show host, number one New York Times best selling author, sought after motivational speaker and one of America's most trusted personal finance experts. Suze now advises her audience to write down and repeat a statement of the reality you want to create, like her favourite affirmation, "I have more money than I will ever need".

HOW AFFIRMATIONS WORK

> *"It's the repetition of affirmations that leads to belief. And once that belief becomes a deep conviction, things start to happen."* ~ Muhammad Ali

Now you know what affirmations are and have created your own personal affirmations, you can make them part of your daily life. They will help reprogram your thought patterns and gradually change your subconscious beliefs. Before we move on to how to use your affirmations let's take a quick look at understanding why and how they work.

NEUROPLASTICITY

Until the 1960s researchers believed that changes in the brain happened in childhood and by early adulthood the brain's physical structure was fixed. However modern research has demonstrated that the brain continues to create new neural pathways and alter existing ones to adapt to new experiences and to learn new information.

The term used to describe this ability of the brain to change and adapt is neuroplasticity, also known as brain plasticity, and it is a wondrous thing indeed. This is huge! It has amazing implications for what were previously assumed to be the natural and somewhat inevitable processes of ageing. And in terms of your *Changeability* it means you are not hardwired to think in certain ways but have the ability to learn new patterns of thought and behaviour.

NEURAL PATHWAYS

> *"As a single footstep will not make a path on the earth, so a single thought will not make a pathway in the mind. To make a deep physical path, we walk again and again. To make a deep mental path, we must think over and over the kind of thoughts we wish to dominate our lives."* ~ Henry David Thoreau

When you learn something new you alter and create neural pathways in your brain. These pathways consist of neurons (nerve cells) in your brain connected through special junctions called synapses.

For example, when you come across a new word, you make new connections between the neurons in your brain to deal with it. These include neurons from the auditory part of your brain to hear the pronunciation, and neurons from your visual cortex to recognize the spelling and so on. Every time you repeat this word to yourself you select and strengthen the connections between the neurons, and the pathway the nerve impulses pass along becomes stronger. With repetition a durable association is created between these neurons resulting in the memory of the word being formed.

Neural pathways are sometimes compared to a forest path. The first person to forge a pathway through the forest has their work cut out. But as more people take the same route the pathway becomes easier to follow, until eventually it is so well worn people walk along it without thinking about it. The same goes for the pathways your thoughts follow.

This means forging the right neural connections into deeply etched neural pathways to support you in achieving your goals. This is where affirmations come in.

So to quickly recap and pull this all together.

- Neuroplasticity means your brain has the ability to learn new patterns of thought.
- It does this through developing new neural pathways.
- This is great news because you want to develop positive empowering self-beliefs.
- Beliefs are repeated patterns of thought that become habits.
- To install your new beliefs you will literally grow each one from a single thought until it becomes a continued pattern of thinking, a belief.
- The most effective way to do this is through repetition.
- Every time you repeat the thought, the neural pathway associated with it becomes stronger.
- With repetition the initial effort of forging the first pathway becomes an easier journey along a familiar path, until it becomes such a well-worn path you don't think about it.
- By this time it's become an established pattern of thought and a belief.

HOW TO USE AFFIRMATIONS

As you start to use your affirmations it's worth noting two ways to make them more effective.

EMOTIONAL IMPACT

The process is accelerated when you add emotional impact by feeling the emotion associated with each affirmation. You know yourself how you recall events more easily that had an emotional impact on you, good or bad.

You want to feel how you would if the affirmation was absolutely true at this time. For example how would you feel if you had all the time to do what you want, or always had more than enough money for the things you want to do – happy, relieved, excited?

If you can get a sense of this feeling as you say or think about your affirmations, the emotional connection to your subconscious has more impact therefore increasing the effectiveness.

REPETITION

As previously mentioned, repetition is key. It's important to consistently implant and reaffirm your affirmations through repetition, and that means going through them every day for a while.

Repetition in quick succession, known as massed practice, is the quickest way to learn something but also the quickest way to forget. Whereas spaced practice, which means repetition at different times throughout the day, brings about slower but longer lasting learning. The ideal is therefore a combination of both, repeating affirmations several times in a row at intervals throughout the day, for fast and longer lasting learning.

The perceived wisdom suggests it takes approximately 30 days to change a habit, including thinking habits. It is therefore advisable to actively use the affirmations for at least 30 continuous days, in order for the subconscious to start accepting your new beliefs and change the underlying limiting behaviours.

Don't be disheartened if it takes longer than 30 days to become ingrained. It takes longer to embed some habits than others, (bad habits seem so much easier to develop than good ones) and is different for each person. A study researching the length of time it took a group of 96 volunteers to develop new habits, concluded it took them an average of 66 days to form the new habits. However there was a big variation in individual times with the shortest time being only 18 days.

Affirmations can also have a much more immediate effect in some cases, with the ability to lift your mood or change the way you are thinking or feeling. They can work as a fantastic pick-me-up and confidence builder and improve your outlook on life. I love affirmations and regularly use them for a range of things both general and specific, depending not only on my goals but also on what I'm doing and how I feel.

Marketing Director Robbie Motter started making affirmations a part of her daily life to see if she could increase her sales leads. Repeating two simple affirmations every day; "People who are interested in doing business with me come into my life every day" and "Each and every day 10 new people order products and/or want to use the service I provide" she saw her personal business explode and now advocates affirmations to increase the marketing results and self-esteem of others.

So let's get to it.

ACTION 4B: HOW TO USE AFFIRMATIONS

Start with this basic technique.

- Go through the personalised empowering affirmations you just created as often as you can. Ideally repeat them several times at intervals throughout the day and at least once a day. Read them out loud and in your head and as you say each affirmation try to get a sense of the emotion of it as if it is already real to you.

- You can use the first, second or third person or a combination of them to describe your own affirmations e.g.
  - I am ...
  - You are ...
  - Kathryn is ...
  - I, Kathryn am now ...
  - You, Kathryn are ...

Here are some more ways to use affirmations. Experiment with them to find which resonate with you.

- Make a recording of your affirmations to play back to yourself. This can be as simple as recording it on your phone or computer.

- Listen to the track several times a day initially (when safe to do so), using a combination of active and passive listening.

- For active listening focus on each affirmation as you hear them, repeating the words out loud or in your head to yourself in the first person, ' I am ...' or add your name 'I, Kathryn am ...' As you say each affirmation get a sense of the emotion of it as if it is already real to you.

- For passive listening have the recording quietly playing in the background without specifically focusing on it e.g. while doing housework, gardening, cooking a meal or walking the dog. Be aware of the affirmations without repeating them or concentrating on them. Your subconscious still hears them and the repetition supplements your active listening sessions. (Please ensure you listen where and when it's safe to do so.)

- Write out your affirmations by hand – either all of them or focus on one at a time. This is particularly useful for where you experience the most resistance to specific statements. Focus on feeling positive, inspired and empowered as you write and make your statements even more powerful by adding how they make you feel to the end of your affirmation (as if it is so). Sitting down and writing out one affirmation repeatedly is an excellent way of focusing your positive attention and powerful intention on what you are affirming.

- Sing or chant your affirmations!

- Write affirmation statements on post-it notes and place them at key strategic points around your house, office or notice board, (e.g. *'I am attractive'* on your mirror, *'I am slim'* on your fridge).

Here's a summary of ways to use affirmations.

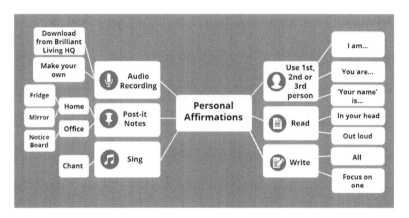

The *Changeability Workout* in the summary chapter near the end of the book shows you how to incorporate affirmations into your daily routine.

RESISTANCE

You may feel a certain amount of emotional resistance to some of your empowering affirmative statements. This is due to a natural fear of change or because an affirmation has a particular resonance for you. Acknowledge the reaction to yourself and then continue with the activity. All of this may feel strange at first but persevere and you will quickly get used to it and start to experience the benefits.

AFFIRMATIONS AND POSITIVE THINKING

Whilst affirmations principally utilize the practice of positive thinking, this is not just a matter of positive thinking in the sense of saying that everything is wonderful and then it will be.

Positive thinking is an important and crucial element of the process but it may not be enough to jump in and start at this point. Using affirmations straight off and in isolation will work sometimes but can create a disconnect or gulf between where you are now and where the affirmation says you are. This is known as cognitive dissonance.

So for example as the positive affirmation is telling you that you have enough money, your negative belief is saying ' oh no I don't!'

This is why I advocate an integrated approach in this mind management programme and ask you to go through all the steps initially.

Of course to begin with it feels false or uncomfortable to tell yourself something you've believed the opposite of for many years, but don't be fazed because you now understand that:

- It's only natural to feel some emotional resistance due to a fear of change and moving out of your comfort zone and perceived safety.
- Just as you developed the old views and beliefs that limited you, you can now develop new thoughts and beliefs to support you.
- You have the power to choose your thoughts.

- Every action starts with a thought, you have to think it first before it becomes real.
- You are telling yourself a new story and writing a new script.
- You have started to feel your way towards your new beliefs with the clearing work on your old negative beliefs in step 3, and the realization that many of the beliefs you held were not actually true.
    - So to return to the money example, you may have had a limiting belief that you will never have enough money. However with the work you did in examining your beliefs your realized it's simply not true to say you know you will definitely never have enough money. This opens up the possibility that there could be a situation where you have more money and even enough money (whatever that means to you). This gives you an altogether different feeling to that engendered by the original belief. It creates optimism and possibility and moves you in the direction of the new belief.

This is the start of your new story and affirmations have a powerful crucial role to play in bringing it to life.

The work you are doing with these mind management techniques is part of a process. It is not a one off event that means one day you wake up with everything changed, a brilliant life and that's it. It's about moving in the right direction and building momentum. Not only that but along the way you are mastering techniques you can use to improve your personal and business life throughout your life and be happier and more fulfilled.

QUICKSTART AFFIRMATIONS

To get going straight away with affirmations or to supplement your own, you can use pre-recorded affirmations. These are available to buy at a reasonable cost from self-development websites such as ours at http://www.brilliantlivinghq.com/ affirmations-products. You can find affirmations with a specific focus or more general ones such as our *Positive Affirmations For Brilliant Living*, which helps affirm new empowering beliefs in key areas of your life including love, work, wealth and health.

You certainly do not need recorded tracks to be successful with this technique, but they do provide a convenient and easy way to immediately access affirmations with minimal effort. And they make you feel good, which can only be a good thing.

11. STEP 5.

VISUALIZATION

SEEING YOUR BRILLIANT LIFE

"Imagination is the beginning of creation. You imagine what you desire, you will what you imagine and at last you create what you will." ~ George Bernard Shaw

The next *Changeability* step is visualization. This goes hand in hand with affirmations. Visualization uses the power of your imagination to create the life you want, so is often called creative visualization. It involves creating a detailed proposal in your mind's eye of what you desire and visualizing it over and over again.

YOU ARE A VISUALIZATION EXPERT

"Imagination is everything. It is the preview of life's coming attractions." ~ Albert Einstein

There is nothing mysterious or unusual in visualization – it's something you do everyday.

Every time you create something new you visualize it in some way before bringing it into being. It's what every poet, artist, musician, architect, engineer, entrepreneur, social and political reformer does prior to making their concept a reality.

But it's not just about big creative enterprises; it applies equally to redecorating your house or making the dinner.

You also use your imagination everyday to paint pictures in your mind of current and future events. You imagine your reactions, feelings and behaviours and predict outcomes (based on your beliefs and experience).

However, as you now know, predicting outcomes perpetuated by limiting beliefs is detrimental to getting the change you want. This is why visualization fits well alongside the empowering affirming beliefs that will transport you to your changed reality.

With this mind management technique you take the visualization you do naturally everyday, enhance it and use it to your advantage in a focused way. You take it to the next level by thinking vibrant thoughts that concentrate on achieving the outcomes you want.

VISUALIZATION IN PRACTICE

In the field of sports psychology visualization is a well-established technique practised alongside goal setting. The elite athlete knows the value of visualization to mentally rehearse his or her fastest race, highest jump, winning game, longest throw (you get the idea). It's a key tool to improve their performance mentally and physically, building belief in their ability to win and training muscle memory.

The runner visualizes running and winning the perfect race over and over so the victory is completely real to them. Going through every intricate detail relating to the scene and performance such as:

- What they see – like the stadium, other competitors and the track ahead.
- Sensations – such as excitement, the surge of adrenalin and the wind on their face.
- What they hear – including the announcements, the starting gun and the roar of the crowd.
- How the race plays out – through the different stages and the victorious finishing line.
- How they feel – powerful, strong, elated, relieved, successful, exhilarated.

They know and believe they can do it because as far as their subconscious is concerned they've won many times before.

I had the pleasure of attending several events at the London 2012 Olympics and Paralympics, where I witnessed a fantastic celebration of human physical and personal achievement. During this time I was struck by the number of athletes who mentioned working with their team's psychologist on strategies to get them in the right frame of mind, including visualization. One British competitor spoke straight after winning a gold medal about how she'd pictured being in exactly this situation and winning the race so many thousands of times she could hardly believe this was the actual real performance and had happened just as she'd imagined it.

Tiger Woods started using visualization techniques from a young age. Forming images in his mind of exactly where he wanted his golf ball to stop, helped him become one of the best golf players in the world. Muhammad Ali would visualize every aspect of his next fight, including the point at which he would knock down his opponent.

Visualization can also impact the physical capacity of the sportsperson, improving muscle performance. Studies indicate that using visualization alongside physical training improves physical performance more efficiently than just training alone. It seems the body reacts to the visualization in a similar way to if the runner was actually running the race, building up the memory of the race within the muscles.

You don't have to be an athlete to test how the body reacts to what you visualize. Imagine taking a juicy bright yellow lemon, cutting it into slices, and placing a slice on your tongue as you smell the fresh citrus aroma and feel the sensation of the tangy sour freshness hit your taste buds.

Chances are you had a physical reaction to this imagined scene, as your mouth started to produce saliva in response to sucking a lemon that was not physically there. The same can work for your favourite foods, such as chocolate, as you imagine the taste and texture when you place the chocolate in your mouth. You set the intention to eat the chocolate and imagine the act and your physiology responds as if you really were eating the chocolate.

MENTAL REHEARSAL

Visualization can be used to create your future in small or big ways, to change beliefs and behaviour, and improve performance.

Visualization is sometimes called *mental rehearsal* and that is exactly what you do. You rehearse in your mind getting the outcome you desire as if it was real now. The more you rehearse it mentally and the more real you make that rehearsal, the more effective this powerful technique is.

Just as an actor rehearses the part, learning lines, adding movement, characterisation, emotion, costume, props, lighting, music, makeup and sound – culminating in the performance where the whole scene is brought to life for the audience – so you are rehearsing to bring your changed life into reality.

WHAT ARE YOU REHEARSING?

So there's great value in rehearsal but what should you be mentally rehearsing? Most visualization techniques focus on imagining the desired outcome. However academic studies suggest it is more effective if you also focus on the process of getting there.

In a study comparing two groups of students, the group who visualized the process required to do well in an exam, e.g. seeing themselves exhibiting good study habits, performed better than the students who solely visualized the desired outcome of good exam grades.

By visualizing how you're going to achieve something, you help to focus your mind on the characteristics and behaviour required to achieve that desired outcome, including what it takes to overcome potential problems and obstacles. If you visualize yourself dealing positively with challenges, you don't have to think about what decision you'll take when you experience it for real. For example, if your goal is to be slimmer, and you visualize yourself politely declining the offer of that slice of Victoria sponge, your less likely to go through the 'shall I, shan't I, it does look good but no I don't think I'll have it', decision making scenario when it happens for real.

Thinking potential challenges through before they occur also has the benefit of setting up the expectation you will achieve your outcome. This move from fantasy to positive expectation increases the effectiveness of visualization according to a 2002 study by Oettingen and Mayer.

Therefore to make the most of this mind management technique, visualize the steps that you will get you there as well as the end outcome. You may not know all the specific steps to take yet, but you can imagine the type of activities the process requires and the characteristics that will help you achieve your goals, so that's what to start with.

MAKING IT REAL

Returning to the acting analogy, just as an actor adds detail and emotion to make a character real and therefore more believable, you want to do the same in your visualization.

Making it real means giving it detail and emotional punch for maximum impact on your subconscious mind. We all recall events more clearly that had an emotional impact on us. The recall is even more powerful when linked to an associated sensation. The sound of a favourite song, the smell of coffee or a baking cake, the touch of a hand, the taste of childhood sweets, these are all examples of sensations with the power to elicit an emotional response.

Through using sensation and positive emotion to get the feeling of what you're visualizing, you imprint your new reality on your subconscious more effectively than words or images alone.

Everything you do starts with a thought, an image in your mind. As you picture the scenes and imagine how you feel, they seep into your subconscious and start to influence your behaviour and the action you take.

As with affirmations you are carving out a neural path to your goals, and the more graphic and emotionally charged the scene, the wider and easier the path becomes to travel along. So the more vivid you make it, the more potent the impact on your subconscious.

You visualize with your conscious mind, but your subconscious mind does not differentiate its response to images that are real and those imagined as real. The subconscious acts in the present moment, so you want to imagine the images as if they're happening now and not in the future. You are convincing your subconscious mind you're already living the life you want, so that your belief system knows it and ensures your conscious mind and senses act in accordance.

You are recalibrating your reality and as far as your subconscious is concerned it will now be its job to look for evidence and opportunities that match this new reality. Remember the filtering role of the reticular formation and activating system, that cluster of neural pathways that function as the search engine of the brain. Through setting a clear intention and focusing on specific images and feelings you help the reticular activating system to perform its job efficiently. You start to see opportunities open up before you and ways to reach your vision become clearer to you.

What you give your attention to, think about most, believe and expect, is what you tend to get, like a self-fulfilling prophecy. So make sure that the present and future you envisage for yourself are what you actually want.

One final point before you get to the visualization action. If what you believe and expect is what you tend to get, then it's worth thinking about how you want to feel when you finish your visualization. For optimum effectiveness you want to cultivate an air of expectancy. In other words whenever you've completed your visualization, go about your day in the knowledge that you fully expect it to materialise in due course, so you don't need to keep thinking about it. Instead you will get on with making it happen (more on that later).

A young Austrian body builder repeatedly visualized what it would be like to win the title of Mr Universe, and then acted as if he had won it. In 1967 the 20 year old Arnold Schwarzenegger won this title for the first of four times and went on to win Mr Olympia seven times and carve out a successful acting career. Likewise, actors Will Smith and Jim Carey actively visualized their success before it became their reality.

But it's not just sports people and actors who benefit from visualization. Carol was unhappy with her weight. It made her feel unattractive and was starting to affect her health. Carol realized that having been overweight for most of her life she only ever thought of herself as fat. So she started to visualize a slimmer, fitter more active version of herself. In her mind's eye she saw herself enjoying shopping for new smaller clothes and looking in the mirror, both activities she normally avoided. She visualized doing what it would take to lose weight and saw herself behaving like a thin person with a healthy relationship with food. A year later Carol was six stones (84lbs) lighter and doing it all for real.

Now it's your turn. You are going to visualize achieving your goals, be they creativity, prosperity, health, love, a fast car, a rewarding career, owning the latest technology, a slender body, emotional peace, satisfying relationships, happiness, enjoyment etc.

Let's start by having a go at the basic visualizing technique before moving on to look at other ways you can enhance your visualization.

ACTION 5A: VISUALIZATION

- Close your eyes and in your mind's eye imagine a scene or series of scenes of how your brilliant life looks and the process of getting there. See yourself doing the things and behaving in the way you need to in order to get the outcomes you want, and see what your life looks like when you've achieved your goals.

- Picture it in the first person as if you are right in the scene yourself at the centre of the action seeing it first-hand, or in the third person as if you are a spectator watching a play or film with you as the main character. Some studies indicate that observing yourself from a third person perspective makes it more likely you'll go on to exhibit similar behaviours. Try both viewpoints to see which comes most naturally to you, and combine the approaches. As you imagine the scenes, make your visualization vivid and emotionally charged.

- See it in high definition and glorious Technicolor with vivid memorable images and bright colours.

- Hear it with a full soundtrack complete with sound effects and music.

- Feel the emotions associated with the images such as happiness, pleasure and excitement.

- Experience the sensations that go with the action like touch, smell and taste.

- Notice the intricate details that make the scene come alive and ring true for you.

- Just as when you watch a play or film you do so in the present moment with the action happening now, imagine your brilliant life as if it exists in the present here and now rather than some future yet to come.

- As with goals and affirmations keep your visualization positive, to imprint the image on your subconscious of what you want rather than what you don't want. Your mind cannot picture a negative; something that is not there. So even though you might imagine the steps you need to take to achieve your goals including setbacks, do not focus on the negative, but emphasize the actions you take and how you overcome difficulties to succeed in the end.

- Take as long as you want with your visualization. You can be flexible from a minute or two up to twenty minutes or more. It should be an enjoyable experience, rather like focused daydreaming with purpose; so don't force it if it doesn't come easily to start. The more you do it the easier and more natural it will become.

Some people like to end their visualization session by thinking or saying something like 'I accept this or something better for the best outcome for all concerned'. This acknowledges there may be a better outcome you are unaware of at this time, and that you want only the best for you and everyone involved.

It might seem a bit paradoxical but visualization doesn't have to be visual. Don't get hung up on whether you can actually see clear accurate images in your mind's eye. People visualize in different ways, from seeing laser sharp images to having a vague awareness of the pictures or what they represent. The important thing is you get a clear sense and feeling for what is happening in the scene being played out in your imagination.

ACTION 5B: CHANGEABILITY VISUALS

You can enhance and reinforce your visualization technique through the use of images. This is a creative and fun addition to your self-development toolkit you can add to your routine any time.

A PICTURE TELLS A THOUSAND WORDS

Create a visual tool to help you focus on and reinforce your visualization by capturing pictorial representations of your vision of your changed life, dreams and goals. It is a picture board or storyboard that tells the story of different aspects of the brilliant life you want. This is sometimes called a vision board, dream board or treasure map.

- Find images, pictures and words in magazines, brochures, on the Internet, or create your own artwork, drawings or photos that capture the essence of what you want to achieve.

- These images might represent relationships and people, such as your ideal partner, yourself or family, or experiences like travel, holidays and hobbies, or possessions, like the car you desire or the type of house you want to live in. They can also be characteristics or features illustrating how you want to live your life such as a healthy lifestyle, or with generosity or enthusiasm.

- Arrange these pictures and words on a board like a notice board. You can cluster them together in categories or randomly display them.

- Place the board in a prominent position so you regularly see it to reinforce what brilliant living means to you, and use it to focus your visualization as you mentally rehearse achieving your goals.

A picture immediately conjures up what can take a whole page of words to evoke. So make the most of it and have some creative fun.

Here are some variations on the picture theme:

- Place your visualization images in a folder or book you can leaf through as you visualize. This works well if you want a mobile or private version of a visuals board.

- Create a visualization folder on your computer containing inspiring images. Use them as an aid to your visualization, e.g. run them as a slow moving slide show.

- Take a photo of your visuals board and use it as
  - the background image on your computer
  - your screensaver

  - the background photo on your mobile phone
  - the screen picture on your iPad, tablet or any other device.

- Create your own screensaver featuring key relevant words, pictures and phrases.

- If you are feeling inspired and adventurous you can create your own storyboard or short video film illustrating facets of your brilliant life.

ACTION 5C: AUDIO VISUALIZATION

The use of audio provides a further creative possibility for your visualization technique.

- The first audio option is to record yourself talking about scenes from your brilliant life. You essentially narrate your way through your visualization from Action 5A. This doesn't need to be a complicated process as it can be recorded on your phone or computer.

- The second option is to use a professionally recorded visualization. You can find these online at a reasonable cost. For example at http://www.brilliantlivinghq.com/ visualization-products we have a guided *Visualization for Brilliant Living* that takes you on a relaxing visualization where you imagine key aspects of your brilliant life. Guided visualizations provide a framework within which to mentally rehearse the achievement of your goals in a structured and timed way, as well as providing a relaxing enjoyable experience.

- Whether you choose to buy a pre-recorded visualization, make your own personal version featuring scenes from your brilliant life, or both; listening to a recording is an effective and convenient way of keeping on track and getting into the habit of visualization.

QUICKSTART VISUALIZATION

Spend 10 minutes daydreaming about what your changed life looks like. Imagine you're in a cinema watching the film of your brilliant life. It's a colourful feel-good blockbuster of the things you did to get where you want to be. There's a great sound track and you're swept along with the experience and emotions of the main character – you. It has a happy ending of what your life is like in your new changed reality.

Visualization works well in conjunction with the other techniques and in the summary chapter near the end you'll find how they all fit together in *Changeability – in summary* and the *Changeability Workout* to incorporate visualization into your daily routine.

12. **STEP 6.**

APPRECIATION

"Appreciation is a wonderful thing. It makes what is excellent in others belong to us as well." ~ Voltaire

It might seem with all this talk of goals and visualization that you'll be living your life in the future, so I want to emphatically state that this programme is not just about looking forward to future happiness. It is also absolutely about where you are now and being happy with who you are and what you have now.

"You must always have a goal in mind, but, as you go along, it costs nothing to stop now and then to enjoy the view around you... As you advance, step by step, you can see a little further into the distance, and take the opportunity to discover things you hadn't even noticed before." ~ Paulo Coelho

When you visualize, you imagine having the changes in place that will move you towards the life you want. Not as an end in itself but in order to change how you feel, live and act, and what you believe about yourself now, which in turn will help you get there.

Step 6 is an amazing mind management technique with the power to change how you feel now and carry you forward. It is the thought practice of *appreciation*.

Appreciation acts as a bridge from the here and now to where you want to be. It puts you in a good place by realising, and feeling great about, all the marvellous things in your present life. This doesn't mean you don't want to make changes in your life, but it puts you in a better place from which to start making those changes whilst living your present life to the full.

Some personal development literature refers to this as raising your vibrational level to a place where it is more in line, or resonates, with your desires. But what this really means is that it makes you feel good now (or better at the very least) in the present moment.

Appreciation makes you mindful of what you have going for you and all the amazing things about you and your life. This puts you in the mood for enhancing and expanding the life you have now from a viewpoint of appreciation for what you have and excitement about what is to come, but not at the expense of the good things you have now.

It's harder to build your *Changeability* and get into a positive mindset to make changes when you are feeling miserable, resentful or desperately unhappy. If you spend a few minutes every day actively thinking about and appreciating the good things in your life, then you reach out for your new life from a position of greater positivity. It is another aspect of turning towards your vision and goals.

ACTION 6A: THE APPRECIATION LIST:

- Write down ten things you are positive about and appreciate in your life today.

- Don't agonise over the list (it's only a start) but just write down the first things that come into your mind. They may be big important things in your life like your partner, children, house, job. Or smaller things, feelings or sensations such as the feel of your dog's fur, or the sound of the birds outside your window in the morning, the taste of freshly baked bread with butter, the warmth of your bath water, or the fact you have hot running water.

- Now read through each item on the list in turn and get a good feeling about it as you think of it.

- Tell yourself a little story about why you appreciate this person, item, situation or sensation, and how it makes you feel. It's like you're sending your appreciation to the item itself, enfolding it with love.
  This is the feeling you want to capture and recapture to put you in a good frame of mind from which to make the changes you want. It's not about getting artificially worked up into a state of superficial positive or motivational thinking, but is an absolutely genuine response based on the evidence of your life.
  You are purposefully evoking this response, so there is

an element of 'fake it till you make it' on those occasions it doesn't come easily and needs enhancing. However this is fine because as you know, the subconscious mind responds to the emotion of what you are feeling and given that the objects and recipients of your appreciation are real, that is certainly more than good enough.

- Write down the 10 items in a notebook, onto paper, or into a new document on your computer.

- Read through your list and add a further 10 items every day for 30 days.

- If you keep this up, by the end of the month you will have 300 things listed that you appreciate about the world and your life. Imagine how you are going to feel as you read through that list. You are so going to be in a totally positive place from which to do your visualization and affirmations and live your life. And you will be truly grounded in the experience of the present moment.

ACTION 6B: DEVELOP THE APPRECIATION HABIT

After kick-starting your appreciation focus it's good to keep it going to make it a habit.

- You can continue the list idea by keeping an appreciation diary or journal on a daily, weekly or

monthly timescale to regularly record what you
appreciate. You might want to make it structured and
give yourself a suggested number of items to write down
per day, week or month. These will soon add up to a
massive list of wonderful things in your life for you to
regularly reflect on.

- A good way to build and maintain the habit is to have
certain times of the day when you consciously think
about what you appreciate. First thing in the morning
and last thing at night as you lay in your bed is a great
way to start the day and set yourself up for the next day.
A daily event such as taking a shower also provides a
great time to reflect on your appreciation list and links
the two daily habits together.

- An effective and convenient way of getting in an
optimum frame of mind for affirmations and
visualization is to listen to a recording that focuses your
thinking on appreciation. You can make your own
recording of items on your appreciation list or use a pre-
recorded one, e.g. http://www.brilliantlivinghq.com/
appreciation-products. This super charges your
appreciation technique through providing appreciative
statements in a quick, easy, convenient format to kick-
start your appreciation habit and make you feel good.

THREE POINTS ON APPRECIATION

"Let us rise up and be thankful, for if we didn't learn a lot today, at least we learned a little, and if we didn't learn a little, at least we didn't get sick, and if we got sick, at least we didn't die; so, let us all be thankful." ~ Buddha

Firstly, if what you focus on is what you tend to get, focusing on the good things about your life (rather than on what's wrong) should bring more positivity and things to appreciate.

Secondly, you can use this technique when you are in a negative frame of mind. To prevent negative thoughts or behaviours spiralling downwards or attracting further similar thoughts, look for some positive aspect of the situation, something, anything, about the situation that you can appreciate, however small or tenuous it might be. Hold on to that thought to halt the negative momentum and gain a slight shift in your perspective, then gradually turn it around by acknowledging more and more positive aspects.

Thirdly, and connected to the first point, it's worth bearing in mind the search engine capability of the reticular activating system. As you compose your list your neural search engine will be on the lookout every day for things you feel positive about. As you purposefully search about, your mental antennae will be poised to pick up the suitable signals and deliver more items to your consciousness to feel good about. As your list gets longer you will find different ways to notice things to appreciate, for instance by focussing in on small details.

APPRECIATION VERSUS GRATITUDE

You may have heard about fostering an attitude of gratitude. This is clearly very similar to appreciation and sometimes the two words are used interchangeably as if they mean the same thing.

It probably doesn't matter which word you use or if you use both, but I have found the notion of appreciation to be most useful. It may just be semantics but to me *appreciation* seems more positive and active in tone.

Gratitude can carry a lingering sense of being grateful (rather than thankful) for what you've got in opposition to what you haven't got, and an undertone of effort or striving. There can also be a sense of having to repay, show or give your gratitude somehow, in return for what it is you're grateful for. On the other hand *appreciation* feels good and is all about what we like and love.

This is why I chose to focus on appreciation in this step, but you might want to mix it up if you make an appreciation recording, to prevent it becoming repetitious. Ultimately it's the sentiment behind the feeling and activity that counts, so use whatever words feel best for you.

QUICKSTART APPRECIATION

A quick way to start your appreciation habit is to grab a pen or your phone right now and note down 10 things you like or appreciate about the world and your life. Just write the first 10 things that come to mind. Don't worry about putting them in order – just write.

13. **STEP 7.**

MINDFUL

MEDITATION

"Learn to be silent. Let your quiet mind listen and absorb."
~ Pythagoras

Earlier we looked at the inner commentary going on in our minds. That almost continuous dialogue of self-talk that reflects and affects what we believe about ourselves, the choices we make, and the actions we take or don't take. We looked at affirmations as a means of replacing this inner dialogue with positive beliefs to empower you to make changes and achieve the life you envisage through your visualization.

This next step greatly enhances the efficacy of these techniques and the whole *Changeability* programme, and provides the bedrock of what will become your *Changeability Workout*. Step 7 is Mindful Meditation.

MINDFULNESS

> *"The Queen said, 'The rule is, jam tomorrow and jam yesterday – but never jam today.'*
> *'It must come sometimes to jam today,' Alice objected.*
> *'No, it can't,' said the Queen 'It's jam every other day. Today isn't any other day, you know."* ~ Lewis Carroll

We started thinking a bit about mindfulness in the previous section on appreciation, noting that being deliberately appreciative makes you mindful of the amazing things you have going for you right now. Not only does it make you aware, it does so in the present, making your *mind full* of appreciation in this moment for what is now, while preparing the way for changes and a brilliant future.

Yet most of the time your mind is not full of appreciation or affirmations, but is going about living everyday life. This normally means it is continually thinking, remembering and planning. You know about this because the mind provides an on-going commentary in the form of mental chatter.

The ability to use the experience of our past to influence our behaviour and to make plans for the future are fantastic developments of evolution, enabling us to become the remarkable beings we are. However these abilities can also be detrimental to our capacity to fully experience the present moment within our lives.

How often do you almost sleepwalk through the activity of your day, except you're not sleeping but time travelling into the past or the future? Or go for a walk through beautiful countryside only to realize at the end you'd hardly noticed your surroundings? Your mind was full of thoughts about what you had to do later, which led to other thoughts about what someone else had done or should have done that they hadn't done, and so on and so forth!

Of course it's good to remember the people we've loved and the experiences from our past that made us who we are today. It's healthy to make plans for the future, indeed this programme uses our ability to manage our minds to set positive goals. However, they should not be at the expense of the ordinary and extraordinary experiences of our present selves.

It isn't always about yesterday or tomorrow – and unlike the White Queen's proclamation to Alice in the quote above, we all need some jam today as well. There is a danger that we spend so much of our time in a negative reliving of past grievances or fretting about what might happen in the future, that we miss out on savouring what is happening right in front of us now.

> "Yesterday is history, Tomorrow a mystery. Today is a gift, that's why it's called the Present."

This popular saying captures the very essence of mindfulness with its recognition that the past is gone and the future not yet here, but we have the present right now to appreciate and live our lives in moment by moment.

> "What day is it?" asked Pooh. "It's today," squeaked Piglet. "My favourite day," said Pooh. ~ A. A. Milne

Mindfulness is about being aware of the here and now and paying attention in a way that is on purpose and non-judgemental.

> "Mindfulness is simply being aware of what is happening

right now without wishing it were different. Enjoying the pleasant without holding on when it changes (which it will). Being with the unpleasant without fearing it will always be this way (which it won't)." ~ James Barez

There is a sense of freedom associated with a timeslot when you're not worrying about the future or concerning yourself with the past, but are instead putting your full mental and physical attention on the present. This is when you experience the feeling of being totally caught up in doing something, that sense of being in the flow or in the zone. It's a habit worth cultivating, even for short periods every day, and one technique that provides the opportunity to do this and more is meditation.

MEDITATION

"Concentrate all your thoughts on the task at hand. The sun's rays do not burn until brought to a focus."
~ Alexander Graham Bell

Meditation in its various forms is practised the world over. It is a feature of the world's great spiritual traditions from Christianity and Judaism to Islam, Hinduism, Taoism, Buddhism and many other faiths. While the specific details vary, the basic underlying steps are similar.

But you don't need to think of meditation in spiritual or religious terms. I mention it here to illustrate the longevity and appeal of meditation as a practice not only through the ages, but across cultures and geographical boundaries.

Today meditation has become part of the mainstream. A national survey for the U.S. Government Department of Health and Human

Services in 2007 estimated over 20 million Americans had used meditation in the previous 12 months. It is becoming increasingly popular amongst the business community as well. A number of Fortune 500 companies, including AOL, Apple and Aetna, offer meditation and mindfulness classes for their employees and the top executives of many major corporations say meditation has made them better leaders. Even the British government has shown interest, with over 95 MPs and parliament staff meeting regularly for mindfulness meditation courses and a Parliamentary all-party group set up in May 2014 to explore the uses of mindfulness meditation.

Meditation is increasingly seen as a success tool with the potential to unlock productivity and creativity. Steve Jobs credited meditation with opening his mind to his innovative ideas, and Albert Einstein spent hours visualizing and mentally performing his experiments whilst in a meditative state. Over 1000 Google employees have been through a company meditation programme and Facebook and Twitter hold in-office meditation sessions and consciously seek to maximize mindfulness within work practices.

That is all very interesting but why am I advocating it as part of the *Changeability* mind management programme?

I'm advocating meditation because it makes you feel better and perform better, and enhances the effectiveness of the other techniques in this system.

Meditation is about attention. This is the common factor across the different traditions and disciplines. It is about focusing concentration in a relaxed way on a particular stimulus such as breathing, chanting, beads, a mantra or picture, rather than being distracted by random thoughts including future plans or past events.

We're going to be mindful of our breathing in this meditation. So if you can breathe and be quiet for a few minutes you can meditate. There is no great mystery to the simple method used here, no right and wrong and with a little bit of practise you can quickly start to experience the benefits of meditation.

Through this simple meditation technique of focusing attention on your breath, you become aware of the nature of the mind to wander. By not judging the mind when it exhibits this tendency, but returning your focus to the breath, you become more aware of your body, your feelings, your thoughts and perceptions and the incessant activity of your mind. Through continually bringing your attention back to your breath you return your focus to the present, rather than dwelling on a past you can't change or worrying about an undetermined future.

THE BENEFITS OF MEDITATION

The potential benefits of meditation include:

- Mindfulness
    - Through focusing on the present and being here now.
- Improved focus, concentration and clarity of thinking
    - Through developing the habit of deliberately applying your attention.
- Engendering a sense of tranquillity, peace and well being
    - Through the refreshing impact of stilling your mind leading to calming of the emotions.

- Developing a deeper self understanding, awareness and acceptance
  - Through overcoming the habit of mental chatter and calming your mind.
- Increased creativity and inspiration
  - Through openness to the subconscious.
- Producing an optimum state to make you receptive to creating change in your life
  - Through reducing your brain wave pattern from your normal everyday beta level of consciousness, to the deeper alpha and theta levels more conducive to deep learning, changes in behaviour and increased moments of insight.

Because meditation leads to states of consciousness more typically associated with brain wave activity found in sleep or moments of deep relaxation, it is an incredibly useful technique to enable you to impress new forms of thought into the subconscious mind. In other words it puts you in a good place from which to undertake other techniques like appreciation, visualization and affirmations. For this reason it will be the first step in your *Changeability Workout* routine, but more of that later.

It's time to meditate.

ACTION 7A: BEGINNING MEDITATION

Read through this action section first before trying it for yourself, as you'll have your eyes closed when you meditate and will not be able to read this!

- Sit quietly and sway or shuffle from side to side a few times to centre yourself.

- Close your eyes. Take a couple of deep calming breaths, letting your shoulders drop as you breathe out. Rest your hands comfortably in your lap and sit in a relaxed upright position with a straight neck and feet on the floor.

- Turn your attention and focus inwards to an awareness of your breath as you breathe in and out.

- Feel the movement of the air passing the base of your nostrils in and out.

- Breathe from the area at the bottom of your rib cage rather than your upper chest, but breathe normally – you don't need to take extra long breaths.

- Concentrate on each breath going in and out.

- Your mind will keep racing with thoughts, don't worry about this; it's part of the point of meditation. Just notice the thought and gently and patiently direct your attention back to the breath moving in and out of your nose.

- Don't follow the train of your thoughts but just let them go as you become aware of them.

- It may help to think of your thoughts as balloons that

you notice and then imagine floating upwards and away, or as thought bubbles that burst as you become aware of them.

- If you find it hard to maintain your focus in this way, you can count your breaths while your mind wanders. Count each in and out breath up to 10 and back, and as you get more used to this type of focus, count just the out breaths. Once you find your mind has stilled more you can drop the counting.

- Start with 5 minutes of meditation per session, and increase the time by a minute a day until you feel comfortable doing 10 minutes or more of meditation at a time.

- Aim for two meditation sessions per day, although once will do if more manageable and is enough to make a difference.

Be gentle on yourself. It is easy to initially feel frustrated by an inability to stop the thoughts coming, but this is to misunderstand the nature of meditation. It is not about controlling the mind but rather about gently focusing your attention. It is not about getting it right or wrong, but is about the process and experience of the practice.

Certainly during my early experience of meditation I was frustrated by my inability to stop my mind racing and constantly planning what I had to do, and I felt like I wasn't doing it right. But after a while I began to realize that these thoughts were all part of the meditation experience, and I found it really helped me to visualize these thoughts floating away. It was also useful to sometimes focus on counting my breaths at the start of a session. Now I look forward to my meditation times, which I find rejuvenating and sometimes enlightening. I also turn to meditation when in need of creative thinking and like to find different peaceful settings or do a walking meditation.

The benefits of meditation are cumulative through regular repetition and practise over time, so try and set aside specific times in the day to invest in yourself. It is worth experimenting with your best times, but many people like to meditate first thing in the morning with a second session later in the day for optimum benefit.

If possible choose an environment free from interruption, ask those around you not to disturb you, find a place of privacy and give yourself a moment away from the phone and computer.

Through regular practise you will gradually discover the benefits of meditation and the beginning of an inner transformation that enables you to fulfil your potential.

As you start your meditation practice you may find it interesting and helpful (particularly if you feel a little reticent) to view the experience as an experiment. Your role in this experiment is to observe what is occurring and feel the processes of the mind and body without interfering with or interpreting what is happening. Noting down your thoughts following meditation can offer considerable insight into your progress.

This is what Julian (as a regular practitioner of this technique) wrote in his journal as he reflected on mindfulness meditation:

"I have found it to be a subtle, yet invaluable tool in the armoury towards achieving brilliant living. It has helped me rediscover the joy of attendance to the here and now, to recognize when my mind is wandering in the process of meditation (oh, I'm having one of those unhelpful thoughts) and how through connecting with my breath I can become more aware of my thought and its impact on my body, feelings and perceptions. It is without exaggeration to say that by consistently practicing and documenting this process I have come to realize that 'for much of my life I haven't really been there'! It has taught me to be more in the present moment; more grounded and has been a genuine life changing and growing experience."

You are not your thoughts and mindful meditation helps you sit back and observe your thoughts as they enter your mind and recognize the sort of thoughts they are and their impact, without self-judgement. It's almost as if you step outside of yourself for a few minutes as an observer. This helps you realize that your thoughts are just your thoughts in that moment, you do not need to be defined by them and can change your reaction to them or let them go.

QUICKSTART MEDITATION

Some people like to follow a guided meditation to help maintain focus on the meditation experience, particularly to begin with. There are many websites where you can find guided meditations including ours at http://www.brilliantlivinghq.com/meditation-products where we have a guided meditation for beginners called *Meditation Moments: With Breath In Mind* with tracks that progress as you develop your meditation practice.

14. **STEP 8. ACTION**

ONE STEP AT A TIME

"Action is the foundational key to all success." ~ Pablo Picasso

It might seem strange to have a step called *Action*, after all isn't that what you've been doing throughout this book. Well yes it's true by reading this book and going through the steps you have of course been taking action, and indeed deserve huge congratulations for getting to this point. However *action* warrants a step of it's own to serve as a call to take the outcomes of all the steps and make them count.

"Thought and theory must precede all salutary action; yet action is nobler in itself than either thought or theory."
~ Virginia Woolf

What's the one thing that differentiates those who read this and think it's interesting from those who change something as a result? They take action.

Action is fundamental to *Changeability*. Through action you change, you turn your dreams and goals into reality and breathe life into the vision of your imagination and the embodiment of your life affirming beliefs. But it's not any old action for the sake of doing something, or action based on negativity or fear. It's action based on and sustained by the new foundations you are building.

- Action born of your vision and goals for your changed life.
- Action grounded in attaining the results of your visualization.
- Action in line with the empowering beliefs of your affirmations.
- Action founded on the energy generated through your appreciation.
- Action centred in your mindfulness of your present experience and making the now count.
- Action stemming from the creativity of your subconscious and implemented with the clarity and focus arising from your meditative practice.

In short it is inspired action for *Changeability*.

Returning to the aha moment from earlier, I was unhappy about my salary and realized I had the power to do something about it, but this would have remained just a thought without action. Mind action combined with tactical action was needed to make it happen. Mind action included the steps we've been through. Setting the goal to get parity of pay, recognizing and exploring potential sabotaging limiting beliefs, and knowing the situation was due to external factors and not a reflection of me as a person. Then affirming empowering beliefs and visualizing the outcome, whilst appreciating the good job and salary I had. Tactical action included gaining the support of colleagues and key people at the top of the organization, timing it to coincide with my release of high profile work, and compiling and presenting a case to HR. All of which resulted in the recognition and increased remuneration for the work we did.

All the examples in this book are of people who followed through with action, otherwise we wouldn't know about them. Harriet Thompson training and running her marathons, Suze Orman leaving her waitressing job, going to work in finance and creating opportunities that led to her TV appearances. David Tootill searching for premises for his mosaics social enterprise and the funding to run it. Arnold Schwarzenegger training for Mr Universe and moving to the USA to pursue his acting dreams. All started with small action steps that led to the fulfilment of their goals.

ACTION 8A: INSPIRED ACTIONS

The important thing is to take action every day towards the changes you want. In Action 8A you decide what those actions are.

This involves breaking your vision goals from Step 1 down into manageable chunks that can be handled one step at a time. These chunks go from milestones, which are interim goals, down to mini-goals which are measurable actions, then right down to micro-steps which are trigger actions. These are the first tiny steps that trigger the next action and make it easier and more likely you'll take it. For example, leaving your gym clothes laid out in your bedroom or your gym shoes by the door, so you don't have to think about getting ready to go straight to the gym when you get up in the morning.

By consistently taking action to achieve these smaller goals you move towards your big goals without overwhelm, strengthened and supported by the mind management techniques you're practicing.

With some goals it's easy to identify the actions to take, e.g. when there's a familiar process to follow, like a training regime for a sporting goal, or an eating programme for a health or weight goal. You may still benefit from researching the best approach for you, and doing that research would be one of your first actions.

> *"Take the first step in faith. You don't have to see the whole staircase, just take the first step."* ~ Dr Martin Luther King Jr.

However, it's possible, even probable, that you don't know the actions to take to get you to your goal, if so it doesn't matter. What does matter is that you start taking the very first small steps along that path. Think around the subject; do a bit of research and make an educated guess about where would be a good place to start.

It doesn't have to be perfect; it's about finding a way in, getting started and building momentum. So let's get started on your inspired actions.

- Taking your vision goals from Step 1, create and write out a milestone or set of milestones for each of them. Milestones are interim goals that make a significant impact towards your overall goal.

- Take each milestone (or interim goal) and think around possible mini-goals and actions to get you nearer to achieving that milestone. Include some trigger actions to get you started. Write down the actions you want to take forward.

- Attach a timescale and relevant measurables to your milestones and actions.

- If you don't know the specific actions to take, just write something fairly broad that can get you started.

What you are doing here is setting your intention and that has a power in itself. Once you get going the momentum will build and the next actions will open up for you.

Whilst the more specific you are, the more focused your action, it's not necessary to write a huge amount of detail. It's a means to an end, not an end in itself. Nor is this a one off exercise, but a living document to be amended and added to as you move towards your goals.

My last boss called me the Queen of Planning. So much so I was asked to write plans for other teams, and put together national plans for businesses links with education and other initiatives. Although I say so myself, I put together some great plans, but in the end it wasn't the quality of the plans that determined whether they produced the goods or not, but the buy-in from those who had to put them into action. Planning for action is key but none of it matters if you don't put your plan into action and follow through on your goals. This step is about ensuring that you do.

Here's part of an action plan to give you the idea, the actions could also be broken down further into smaller chunks.

INSPIRED ACTIONS		
Actions	**Milestone**	**Vision and goals**
Get all bank statements and financial documents in one place (1 day – target date)	*Credit cards fully paid (in one year – date)*	*I have financial freedom*
Research options for consolidating cards, compare monthly rate, agree and action best deal (1 week – target date)		
Identify and put into action one-off ways to get more cash e.g. selling things I don't need at car boot sale, e-bay, etc. (1 month – target date)		

Look out and prepare for promotion opportunities at work, or seek and find another job that pays more, or an additional stream of income (6 months – target date)		

The actual process of writing down your goals and creating a list of actions is hugely helpful as it directs your focus, (and energy follows focus,) and clearly states your intent. This sends a message to your subconscious mind to look for and notice the opportunities your positive action generates. The communication on this may not always be obvious so be open to unexpected incidents and coincidences and listen for your intuition.

You have now created an action plan. The beauty of an action plan is it provides a way to manage your mind in a different context. You don't have to keep thinking about your next step or what you can do today to work towards what you want to change or achieve. It makes procrastination less likely as you know exactly what you can do to get on with it.

This is another reason it's so helpful to break your goals, milestones and actions down into small doable sizes. If you go to your action plan and see what looks like an insurmountable mountain to climb you will find a load of things to do other than what you should be doing. Whereas if your plan has a defined manageable action to take, with the expectation it leads to the next one, and even better a timescale or deadline attached to it, you are more motivated to do it.

This then brings its rewards in terms of achievement (including a dopamine rush). More about that in the last two steps but first some hints on taking action.

ACTION 8B: ACTION ON ACTION

Now that you've identified the key actions to get you started, it's time to take action on your actions.

As you take that action here are five daily action points to bear in mind and keep you going.

- Take positive consistent action every day.
- Keep up the action of your *Changeability Workout.* (These are the techniques suitable for daily use: meditation, visualization, affirmations and appreciation. More on this is in the summary chapter at the end of the book.)
- When you feel stuck – take action, do something, even just a tiny action or gentle self-talk, to get your energy moving
- When you experience self-defeating self-sabotaging thoughts, take away their power:
  - Stay engaged in the present moment. Don't let your mind follow a train of thought laying out some imagined future negative scenario.
  - Do something positive towards achieving what you want or at least take some action, such as

going for a walk, to distract you from the negative thinking. We all experience the fear of not being good enough when we take a new direction or try a new venture. But success comes to those who take action and don't let fear stop them. Not only is there then less opportunity for unhelpful fearful thoughts to get through, but the action moves you closer to achieving the change you want.

- And really importantly – ask yourself the following questions every day:
    - Does my action today support my goals?
    - Is my behaviour taking me nearer to my goals or away from them?
    - And if not – change it! You have the Changeability!

I have summarised these into what I call my *5-a-day Manifesto for Action* at the end of this section below. You might like to print it out from the worksheets or make your own version and display it in a prominent place, to encourage you to take positive action every day.

QUICKSTART ACTION

Ask yourself what action you're taking today towards your goals and is it helping you change what you want to change.

5-A-DAY MANIFESTO FOR ACTION

1. *I take positive consistent action every day.*

2. *I keep up the action of my Changeability workout routine.*

3. *If I feel stuck I take action, however small, to get my energy moving.*

4. *If I experience self-sabotaging thoughts I stay engaged in the present moment and do something positive towards achieving my desires.*

5. *I ask myself everyday:*

– Is my behaviour taking me nearer to my goals?

– Does my action today support my vision and goals?

15. STEP 9.

ACCOUNTABILITY

"The ancient Romans had a tradition: whenever one of their engineers constructed an arch, as the capstone was hoisted into place, the engineer assumed accountability for his work in the most profound way possible: He stood under the arch." ~ Michael Armstrong

You are well on the way now – your *Changeability* increasing with every step.

You know what you want, and you're installing the beliefs that are creating the behaviours that will get the results you want. You're experiencing the benefits of meditation, are living life in the moment and appreciating what you have now. It's making you feel good and helping you get more to be appreciative of. You are taking action every day to make the changes you want to see in your life.

What is going to keep you on the path? What is going to motivate you when events happen to throw you off course, or you reach a plateau, or feel you're not getting nearer your goals?

- First, you're going to remember why you wanted to make this change, and how achieving it is going to feel as you take action and when you get there.
- Second, you're going to look at what you are saying to yourself and what lies behind it. Are negative unhelpful beliefs influencing your invisible script and if so you know what to do to address them (hint; revisit steps 2 and 3).
- Third, you are going to find a way of making yourself accountable for your actions and goals.

Don't worry if this sounds daunting or dull – it needn't be.

Accountability is really just about taking responsibility for your goals and actions and being answerable to someone for them. It is about 'putting it out there' in some way that improves your motivation and focus. This can be in a big public way or a small more private way, depending on your temperament and circumstance.

> *"Accountability separates the wishers in life from the action-takers that care enough about their future to account for their daily actions."* ~ John Di Lemme

Accountability improves your chances of success. Just look around you to see examples of accountability in action. Why do people pay weight loss companies to go and get weighed every week when they could easily do it themselves at home for free?

Remember Carol, the lady who used visualization to help her lose 84lbs. Visualization helped Carol get in the right mindset to be slimmer but that alone wasn't enough to shift the pounds. Carol also took action to eat differently and take exercise, but it was her weekly trip to the local slimming club that kept Carol motivated to keep going until she achieved her weight goal.

There Carol received information and tips about food to help her. After a while she knew what to do and would occasionally even skip the talk and just go to get weighed. But Carol kept going week in week out. Why did Carol, and thousands of others like her keep going? They go because of the accountability factor, because knowing someone (or a group) is going to know whether they have lost weight this week or not helps to keep them on track. They go because the praise and recognition motivates them when things are going well and supports and encourages them on those weeks when the scales don't move (or not in the right direction).

Accountability is part of the appeal of having a coach or mentor. The instruction and advice element is important but so is the accountability factor, knowing that you will be reporting back on the outcome of strategies pursued and progress made.

In July 2013 Julian and I flew 5000 miles to California to meet up with a group of 25 people we'd never met before, as part of the first ever 1Day Business Breakthrough Mastermind run by online entrepreneurs Pat Flynn and Chris Ducker. It was exciting, fun, challenging and a little scary as it was the first time we'd presented our new enterprise of BrilliantLivingHQ.com to anyone, let alone a group of entrepreneurs including Pat and Chris!

So why put ourselves through the expense and challenge? You

know the answer of course – it was accountability. From the moment we took action and grabbed our place on that group, we had a deadline. We knew in two months time we'd be standing up in front of this group to show our website and talk about the Brilliant Living Blueprint programme we were creating. So they had to be sufficiently developed for us to talk about them and get useful feedback. And they were, even though we were putting the finishing touches to them 2 hours before we left for Heathrow Airport and still had to pack!

It gave me an insight into the value of Mastermind groups, and I continue to be part of a couple of Mastermind groups. I've also experienced at first hand the benefits of group and individual coaching and mentoring, including getting this book completed and out there.

In these examples the personal accountability element is combined with the support offered by the other party. This is an ideal combination and not to be underestimated.

Of course you don't have to tell anyone about your vision, aspirations and action. You can be accountable to yourself, get your support from reading this, using some audio products, visiting websites like http://www.brilliantlivinghq.com and wait for the results to speak for themselves. You can make changes and achieve your goals like this but you would be missing out on a valuable tool with the potential to significantly increase your success.

So let's assume that as you're smart you're going to do everything you can to assure your success and fully participate in Step 9.

ACTION 9A: BEING ACCOUNTABLE

- Decide how you are going to be accountable.
  Accountability in this context revolves around telling
  someone about what you are doing. Here are some
  suggestions:
    - Tell a friend, colleague, partner, or family
      member. Although accountability sounds rather
      formal it could be as simple and informal as
      sharing your goal and timescale in a
      conversation with a friend, colleague or
      relative, and then discussing how you are
      getting on in future conversations. (You can of
      course do the same for them and their goals.)
    - Have a more formal arrangement through using
      a mentor or coach.
    - Join or start a Mastermind group. This is a
      likeminded group of individuals who meet or
      communicate regularly online or in person to
      share ideas and provide challenge, support and
      accountability to each other.
    - If going public about your goals will motivate
      you, record a video of yourself talking about
      your vision and goals and the changes you
      want to make and put it on YouTube.
    - Use an app like *Lift* for daily motivation,
      coaching and prompting in an online social
      context (for iPhone or web from lift.do)

- Join the Changeability Facebook Group and share your goals and progress.

- Share your goals, milestones, actions and key dates with your accountability partner or group.

- Provide an update on progress and get feedback and support for your next actions.

- If helpful and appropriate, structure and record the accountability conversation in writing or on video or audio. Here's an example of a structured approach.

MY ACCOUNTABILITY CHART			
Who I am accountable to	Actions, milestones, goals and key dates shared	Update on progress on actions, milestones and goals	Feedback, comments, next actions and review date
...	...	...	...

Being accountable for your goals will significantly improve your performance and is a key tool used by many of the most successful people in the world. You too can experience its power by finding someone today to be accountable to.

QUICKSTART ACCOUNTABILITY

Phone a friend today and tell them about one of your goals. Tell them what action you're taking this week towards it and that you'll talk to them in a week's time to let them know how you've got on.

16. **STEP 10.**

REFLECTION AND

CELEBRATION

"The unexamined life is not worth living." ~ Socrates

You're amazing. You've made it to the last *Changeability* step.

Most of the techniques have involved looking forward in some way to your changed brilliant life or taking action in the present. This final step includes a bit of both but also provides an opportunity to look back on what you've done.

We sometimes get so focused on action – doing, doing, doing – and rushing headlong into the next thing on our plan that we lose valuable insights and increased motivation from what we have already done. Hence the final step of *Reflection*. And yes it might look like I sneaked in an extra step here but I'm claiming that *Celebration* is part of reflection as you will see.

THE VALUE OF REVIEW

> *"Knowing yourself is the beginning of all wisdom."*
> ~ Aristotle

It's worth reflecting on your experience of the *Changeability* programme and progress made towards your goals. This could be a formal process as part of your accountability setup or an informal personal review. Find what works for you, from a brief regular round up to a fuller review at set intervals.

Don't get hung up on the process. The benefit is in the reflection and what you take from it to inform your future action. And whilst it's helpful to briefly jot down key points, this is a thought process not a form-filling exercise.

As you think about how you're getting on with your goals and your *Changeability*, you will recognize what has worked well and what hasn't worked so well for you.

THE VALUE OF SETBACKS

Turning first to what might not be working well for you at this point. Whatever else, do not beat yourself up if you don't achieve your goals in the timescale you set yourself or have a slip or two along the way. Just because you receive the odd set back doesn't mean you should abandon your goals or that you've failed in some way.

> *"I have not failed 10,000 times. I have not failed once. I have succeeded in proving that those 10,000 ways will not work. When I have eliminated the ways that will not work, I will find the way that will work."* ~ Thomas Edison

It's feedback not failure, as this famous quote from Edison illustrates about the ten thousand prototypes it took him to develop a commercially viable light bulb.

It is about understanding what's holding you back or getting in the way of achieving what you thought you could achieve. It is about understanding why things haven't gone as you planned and, crucially, how to do things differently from now on to improve the outcome. It is about finding out that the way you did it was not the best way and having the flexibility to tweak it or try a new approach. In other words it is about learning from this experience how you can use it to your future advantage.

Let's go back to the notion of perception here. It is about how you perceive the situation, which is tied up with your beliefs about the world and yourself.

When you first attempted to ride a bike you wobbled and maybe fell off, but you didn't see this as failure and give up. You believed could ride a bike as you saw lots of other people doing it. You learnt from the experience how to modify what you were doing to balance better and with practise perfected your technique.

So when your actions don't go to plan, reflect, take the positive learning and modify them, and if necessary, the milestones and goal itself.

THE VALUE OF SUCCESS

> "The more you praise and celebrate your life, the more there is in life to celebrate." ~ Oprah Winfrey

It is equally important to reflect on and celebrate your success. To recognize what is working well for you and why, and whether there is something you can take from it to inspire or replicate in other actions and goals.

We are all motivated by our successes so it's imperative to give yourself multiple opportunities to be successful. Notice the small wins along the way. Having broken your goals down into milestones and actions, each of these presents the chance to mark up a success. Don't pass the opportunity by; they are important for reinforcing the changes you are making in your life.

These can be small actions that signify you've achieved something. It can be as simple as making a list of actions for the day or week and ticking them off as you complete them, and great for giving you that feeling of getting on and making progress.

Use little rewards, such as going for a walk or reading a book, to help organize and encourage you to complete an activity. When I finish writing this paragraph I'm going to have a cup of tea!

And of course achievement of key milestones or overall goals deserves a special celebration of some sort.

A good way of doing this is to record your achievements as you go along e.g. in your journal. If you are using a visual representation of your changed life like a vision or dream board, move the items you've achieved to an 'achieved', 'accomplished' or 'I did it!' area or use a separate board or folder. You will be amazed, gratified and encouraged as you look back on what you have done.

As with the appreciation technique, noticing your wins (however small) has a cumulative effect where you increasingly look for and find success.

There are many ways of doing this so find what suits you best, but the details of how you do this are not as important as the fact you do it. The critical point here is to recognize your successes to reinforce the behaviours and beliefs that delivered them, increase your confidence in the process, bring you further wins and maintain your momentum in making the changes you want – and have some fun along the way.

ACTION 10A: REFLECT AND CELEBRATE

- Review your actions and progress towards your goals at regular intervals.

- Revisit your *Satisfaction with life – Starter for 10* list or chart from Action 1A to measure movement.

- Modify your actions, milestones or goals in the light of your experience so far.

- Reward your small wins and celebrate your successes.

- Use the *Reflection and Celebration checklist* below to reflect on progress and success with specific goals and your experience of the process. There are 17 questions, all slightly different but some similar, so you don't need to go through them all every time, but rather use the ones that appeal most or bring something to mind as you read them.

- Share your experience and successes.

REFLECTION AND CELEBRATION CHECKLIST

ABOUT YOUR GOAL:

- Describe what has changed since you first began your goal (e.g. different activities you undertake since you started this goal, increased confidence, etc.).
- What is the best thing that happened this week/month; something someone said or did, something you said or did, a feeling, an insight, or a mini-goal or action accomplished.
- What's the most difficult part of achieving your goal?
- If you were giving advice to someone trying to achieve this goal and they had got this far, what would you advise them to do?

ABOUT THE EXPERIENCE AND PROCESS:

- Are affirmations, meditation, visualization, appreciation and goal setting a part of your daily routine? If not, how could you gradually increase the use of these mind management techniques and tools for change?
- What changes have you noticed about the way you think about yourself?
- What do you feel are the main things you have learnt on this journey?
- If you could travel back in time to the first day of your *Changeability* journey, what would you tell yourself about the trip so far?

- What have you done or someone has said to you that surprised you since starting this book? Why?
- What compliments have you been given and what did they mean to you? How did you react? What about criticism and your reaction to it?
- What did you do this week or month that made you proud? Why?
- What insights have you gained from this experience?
- What advice would you give to someone embarking on their own *Changeability* quest?
- Think back on a moment when you felt especially happy or satisfied in this programme. What does that tell you about yourself?
- Write and date something you have learned about yourself as a result of this experience.

CELEBRATION

- How have you celebrated your achievements so far?
- What have you got planned for your next celebration?

QUICKSTART REFLECTION AND CELEBRATION

One simple quick way to get started with reflection and celebration is to just ask yourself what you've done today to make you feel proud and why. Write it down. It only takes a moment so you can do it right now.

Well done – that's fantastic!

17. **WHAT NEXT?**

This book has given you a ten-step blueprint for the *Changeability* to make the changes you want. As you take the basic design of the *Changeability* mind management programme and make it your own through your actions, part of your focus will be on the destination ahead of achieving your goals and part will be on appreciating and enjoying life in the present, which is after all the only time you have to take action in.

This is the notion of the journey being as important as the destination. Truly brilliant living is about having a balanced approach. It is about finding equilibrium between moving towards your changed life through the goals that give you drive, direction and a sense of purpose, and enjoying and appreciating the life you have now.

HAPPINESS

When you ask people what they want out of life, most say the main thing they want is to be happy. Of course the big question is what makes you happy.

There are experiences that make you feel happy. Things you love doing, maybe having a great night out with friends, bungee jumping, enjoying a film at the cinema, lying by a pool in the Caribbean. This sort of happiness is tied up with the notion of pleasure, enjoyment and fun.

Then there is a more fundamental type of happiness that is more of a state of being. This sort of happiness comes from being content with yourself and comfortable in your own skin. It's about being happy in yourself without relying on other people or external props. It's not about the highs of life but about everyday and the wellbeing that builds resilience and confidence, and helps you meet the inevitable challenges of life. It doesn't mean you don't want more happy experiences or to improve your life in some way, but that there is a basic contentment and satisfaction at the heart of you.

Happiness is not an endpoint, something to be achieved once and for all. Happiness is an attitude, approach and habit, and a by-product of living well.

Likewise this is not about some future happiness that will be yours when you change, or get more money, or lose weight, or achieve any particular goal.

It's not that you wont be happy to achieve your goals or attain whatever it is you desire, but that when you find a way to be happy and satisfied now, you are more likely to accomplish your intentions.

Brilliant living is about being joyful and happy now whilst at the same time looking forward with optimism and purpose, knowing you have *Changeability*.

INSPIRATION

"People who seek only success rarely find it, because success is not an end in itself, but a consequence." ~ Paulo Coelho

As you use this programme to make changes in your life, you will create new visions and goals to aim for while you appreciate and enjoy the fruits of your progress so far.

In this and everything you do it's good to be mindful of what lies behind your vision of brilliant living. The goals and actions you feel happy about and inspired by are those aligned with your values and purpose. Your commitment, action and focus is driven by what motivates you. This is all about the 'why' behind what you're doing, whom you're doing it for and who will benefit.

The wonderful thing about taking charge of your brilliant life is that it not only changes your life, but has a positive impact on those around you, your family, friends, colleagues and community.

What an amazing inspirational effect you are about to have!

18. **SUMMARY**

"Knowing is not enough, we must apply. Willing is not enough, we must do." ~ Johann Wolfgang von Goethe

This chapter gives you summaries of what you've read, to place it all into context and make it simple to see what to do next. But first some words on putting yourself first.

YOU ARE YOUR PRIORITY

Personal development and change are not easy to achieve. They require commitment and action – but the rewards are great. Remind yourself of this at times when other priorities crowd in on you.

We all lead busy lives and make choices about how to use our time, so if you feel you haven't got time to prioritize yourself, think again. Examine how you spend your time, identify your non-productive activities and replace them with productive ones such as the daily workout, think again about what you want out of life and why, and commit to making it happen.

You have in your hands right now the very means to make it happen. So go ahead – and change your life.

DAILY ROUTINE

As you worked through the *Changeability* programme you'll have noticed that whilst some techniques and activities are designed for specific stages like the beginning or end of the programme, others can be used on a daily basis for maximum efficacy.

This is my suggested formula for your daily workout routine. There is however no absolute right or wrong way to use these techniques, but this combination benefits from the cumulative effect of a regular routine.

CHANGEABILITY WORKOUT

MEDITATION

Meditation provides a good starting point as it brings your mind and body into the present moment, focuses your attention, relaxes you, and enhances your awareness. So it's a good idea to begin your daily workout or routine with a few minutes of meditation. This can be by yourself or using a guided meditation. You may like to meditate two or three times in a day as you start to experience the benefits.

Start with 5 minutes gradually increasing to between 10-20 minutes.

VISUALIZATION

Follow your meditation by mentally rehearsing achieving your goals and living your vision in a vivid and emotionally charged visualization, enhanced and inspired by any visual props you've created.

Time: 5-10 minutes.

AFFIRMATIONS

Having rehearsed your changed brilliant life, it's now a good time to install and affirm the positive self-beliefs that will influence your thinking, behaviour and actions to get you where you want to be. Input your personal affirmations using your preferred methods.

Time: 5-10 minutes.

APPRECIATION

Finish off your daily workout routine with a healthy dose of appreciation. This builds on the positivity generated by the affirmations you've just done, and roots the whole routine in the positive reality of the here and now in an uplifting and energising way. Use your appreciation list or journal to focus on what you appreciate in life, and in doing so put you in a feel good place poised for action.

Time: 3-5 minutes.

Reap the rewards of your daily workout routine by taking daily action towards your goals and vision

Time: However long it takes.

As you get familiar with the activities and format find what suits your lifestyle and preference, including the order of activities and time allocated. All can be used individually.

You may find it challenging to fit in 20 or 30 minutes for your *Changeability* workout in one block every day, if so split up the activities throughout the day. Or try working through the routine but pay particular focus to one element by repeating it at intervals through the day. If for example you are working on specific self-beliefs, you repeat your affirmations 2 or 3 times a day for a month or two.

So follow the format or experiment to find what works best for you.

CHANGEABILITY – IN SUMMARY

This *Changeability Summary* table brings together all the techniques and actions used throughout the book and summarises them for your convenience. You can clearly see the rationale for them and when to do them as well as how they fit together and build on one another.

VISION SETTING		
Why	When	How
To define your desires and create a vision for your changed brilliant life and the goals to take you there	Once at the start	1A: Rate the satisfaction with key areas in your life to identify where you most want to make changes 1B: Capture what your changed life looks like; your vision of success 1C: Define your desires and craft your goals based on your starter for 10, your vision and the 5Ps of *Changeability* goals

TAKING STOCK		
Why	When	How
To identify the underlying beliefs and thought habits that potentially sabotage change and your route to living the life you want	Once following action 1	2A: Listen to your inner voice while comparing the desires and goals from 1C with your present life reality, to capture the self-beliefs that limit your growth and achievement

CLEARING THE GROUND		
Why	When	How
To recognize negative self-limiting beliefs for what they are and let them go	Once following action 2 (to be repeated if required)	3A: Examine the self-beliefs identified in 2A to recognize the unhelpful, untruthful, limiting set of thoughts that block progress to change and your brilliant life 3B: Clear away these negative limiting beliefs, releasing them from your mind through the power of your conscious thought and imagination 3C: Reinforce 3B through physical symbolic actions

AFFIRMATIONS		
Why	When	How
To influence your subconscious to recalibrate your beliefs and expectations and powerfully change your thoughts, behaviour and life	Once following action 3Daily – at least once per day for as long as required (minimum 30 to 90 consecutive days and then as desired)	4A: Create your personal affirmations by transforming the limiting beliefs of 2A into the empowering beliefs needed to transport you to the vision and goals of 1C 4B: Programme in your personal affirmations through your preferred methods such as reading, writing, singing, recording and listening.

VISUALIZATION		
Why	When	How
To use the power of your imagination to mentally rehearse achieving your desired outcomes	Daily For as long as desired	5A: Visualize yourself achieving your goals and living your vision 5B: Create *Changeability* visuals using images to enhance and inspire your visualization experience 5C: Record and listen to your visualization. and/ or a pre-recorded visualization to guide your visualization of key aspects of your ideal life

APPRECIATION		
Why	When	How
To appreciate the good things in your life now, ideally positioning you to start making changes whilst living your present life to the full	Daily or as often as possible	6A: Compile your appreciation list and feel the emotion of your response, starting with 10 items and building up over time in an appreciation notebook or journal 6B: Develop the appreciation habit using a diary, linking it to daily habits and recording your list

MINDFUL MEDITATION		
Why	When	How
To enhance your experience of the present moment, improve focus and increase wellbeing, self-awareness, creativity and the effectiveness of the other techniques	Daily (ideally twice per day)	7A: Sit still with closed eyes, focus on your breath going in and out, notice the thoughts that come, let them go and bring your attention back to your breathing to practise a basic mindfulness meditation technique

ACTION		
Why	When	How
To turn your goals into reality and breathe life into the vision of your imagination and the embodiment of your life affirming beliefs	Daily until change achieved	8A: Create your personal action plan inspired by the vision and goals of step 1, the affirming beliefs of step 4, the visualization of step 5, the appreciation in step 6, and the meditative habit of step 7. Outline the key actions you will take and milestones on route to your goals 8B: Copy or print the *'5-a-day manifesto for action'*, place it in a prominent place and apply what it says, every day

ACCOUNTABILITY		
Why	When	How
To take responsibility for your goals and actions and be answerable to someone for them, to significantly improve your performance and success	Initially and then on-going as required	9A: Decide how you will be accountable and to whom, record it on the *My accountability chart* and put it into action, share your goals, discuss your progress, get feedback and support

REFLECTION AND CELEBRATION		
Why	When	How
To reflect on the *Changeability* programme and experience, and progress made towards goals, learn from it and celebrate successes along the way.	Periodically and when milestone or goal achieved	10A: Review progress towards your goals to see what is working well and what needs modifying and change accordingly. Take every possible opportunity to celebrate your successes, however small or significant.

WHAT YOU'VE ACHIEVED (IN UNDER 200 WORDS)

Through the *Changeability* programme you've:

Created your vision of brilliant living and set your goals. Looked at your present life to identify the beliefs, thoughts and habits that limit you and get in the way of you reaching your goals. Cleared these inhibiting thoughts and beliefs away and are replacing them with empowering thoughts and beliefs through positive affirmations. Bringing your vision of brilliant living to life through the power of visualization – seeing it, feeling it, living it. At the same time getting into the optimum frame of mind for happiness now and attracting the future life you want, through appreciation of the wonderful things about your life now. Practicing meditation to improve your focus, open up your subconscious to accept new empowering beliefs, and improve your life in general! Using the energy, focus, impetus, motivation and inspiration that your new beliefs and vision give you, to take action every day, grab the new opportunities you now see, commit to accountability and make things happen. Making the change, achieving the goal and celebrating big time. Being happy now as you look forward to your next new goals. This is brilliant living. Enjoy it!

19. FINAL THOUGHTS

"You have brains in your head.
You have feet in your shoes.
You can steer yourself in any direction you choose.
You're on your own.
And you know what you know.
You are the guy who'll decide where to go." ~ Dr Seuss

Congratulations! You have reached the end and that is great news because the time has come to take massive action. You now know what you need to know to start making the changes you want to make and live the brilliant life you want.

You know that if you think the thoughts you've always thought, tell yourself the things you've always told yourself and do things the way you've always done them, that you will get what you've always got. That is why you're now prepared to let go and to make that bold step in a new direction.

You know you now have the techniques and tools to empower you and the ability to make this change.

Whilst others might be daunted, you can feel invigorated, excited and alive to the endless opportunities the world has waiting for you to reach out and take.

Here's to your *Changeability* and your brilliant life!

20. KEEP IN TOUCH

I would love to hear your stories and examples of using the *Changeability* programme or any of the techniques in it. And don't forget to join our free private Changeability Facebook Group.

Facebook Group: facebook.com/groups/Changeability

Website: brilliantlivinghq.com

Podcast: changeability.me/podcast

Facebook Page: facebook.com/BrilliantLivingHQ

Twitter: twitter.com/brilliantlvnghq

Worksheets: brilliantlivinghq.com/changeabilityws

Email: Kathryn@BrilliantLivingHQ.com

Changeability website: changeability.me

ENDNOTES

INTRODUCTION

Johnson, S. M.D. *Who Moved My Cheese,* 1998, Vermilion London p.72

YOUR CHANGED LIFE

Cecil Alec Mace (1894–1971) was a pioneer in advancing British industrial psychology during the inter-war period. In 1935, Mace conducted the first experimental studies of goal setting and in the following years set out many of the basic principles that are taught today. From the article, '*Cecil Alec Mace: The man who discovered goal-setting*' International Journal of Public Administration, Vol 17, Issue 9, 1994

Edwin Locke studied the processes and results of goal setting within organizations for over 40 years. In their 1981 review of laboratory and field studies on the effects of setting goals when performing a task, Locke *et al* concluded that 'goals affect performance by directing attention, mobilizing effort, increasing persistence, and motivating strategy development' [i.e. different ways of achieving the goal]. Locke, E. A., et al (1981) Goal Setting and Task Performance: 1969 to 1980. Psychological Bulletin, Vol. 90, No. 1, pp.125–152

THE BRILLIANT YOU

Scott Peck, M. *The Road Less Travelled,* 1978 Arrow Books, p.270

The flea riding on an elephant analogy is described by Pratt, G. Ph.D. and Lambrou, P. Ph.D. *Code To Joy*, 2012, Harper Collins, pp.77-85

George A. Miller, (1956) Harvard University, The Magical Number Seven, Plus or Minus Two: Some Limits on our Capacity for Processing Information, First published in *Psychological Review, 63*, pp.81-97.

The reticular formation is described by David Darling in 'The Encyclopaedia of Science' (at DavidDarling.info) as *'a network of nerve pathways and nuclei throughout the brainstem connecting motor nerves and sensory nerves to and from the spinal cord, the cerebellum, and the cerebrum. It is estimated that a single neuron in this network may have synapses with a many as 25,000 other neurons.'*

The RAS is a part of the brain that forms a special system of nerve cells linking the medulla, pons, midbrain, and cerebral cortex. The RAS functions as a sentry. In a noisy crowd, for example, the RAS alerts a person when a friend speaks and enables that person to ignore other sounds. Taken from the article *Visualize* in encyclopedia.com.

This 'Unknown unknowns' statement was made by Donald Rumsfeld, United States Secretary of Defense, on February 12, 2002 at a press conference concerning the Iraq war. The subject matter is not the point here but rather the notion that there are things we don't know that we don't know about and are therefore outside of our sphere of experience.

YOUR BRILLIANT THOUGHTS

Prince Siddhartha Gautama Buddha, 563 BCE to 483 BCE

Lipton, B. *The Biology of Belief,* Elite Books, 2005, p.30

Amen, D. G. *Change Your Brain Change Your Body,* Piatkus, 2011, p.232

Functional magnetic resonance imaging technology (fMRI) is used to look at the anatomy of the brain and SPECT (single photon emission computed tomography) imaging looks at blood flow and activity patterns to see how the brain functions.

Dr Amen cites two studies in which researchers had demonstrated the different effects that specific types of thoughts notably happy and sad thoughts had on the brain activity of the participants, in Amen, D. G. *Change Your Brain Change Your Body,* Piatkus, 2011, p.232

TAKING THE CONTROLS

It's interesting to think where many of us got the idea that life should be fair in some way despite much evidence to the contrary. Mostly from our parents or teachers telling us to be fair, or from the stories we were told where the hero always triumphs and the prince gets his princess. This is not an argument for not playing fair, or not wanting a fairer world, but rather an observation.

I am not referring to actual victims here in the sense e.g. of being a victim of crime etc.

Please note these comments are intended as general examples and are not necessarily applicable where certain medical conditions exist such as clinical depression. Whilst some of the techniques offered, such as meditation, can be helpful, medical advice should always be sought before undertaking any programme.

Pratt, G. and Lambrou, P. *Code To Joy,* 2012, Harper Collins, p.137

STEP 1. VISION SETTING

Lewis Carroll, *Alice's Adventures in Wonderland,* 1865, Chapter 6

Gawain, S. *Creative Visualization,* 2002, Nataraj Publishing, p.136

Dr Peters, S. *The Chimp Paradox,* 2012, Vermilion, p.41

STEP 4. POSITIVE AFFIRMATIONS: CREATING EMPOWERING SELF-BELIEFS

Opening affirmation quote is by Abbey Gaines, *Married by Mistake,* 2009

Kendra Cherry, *'What is Brain Plasticity?'*

http://psychology.about.com/od/biopsychology/f/brain-plasticity.htm

Lally, P. and Van Jaarsveld, CHM. and Potts, HWW. and Wardle, J. (2010) 'How are habits formed: Modelling habit formation in the real world.' *EUR J SOC PSYCHOL* , 40 (6) 998 – 1009

STEP 5. VISUALIZATION: SEEING YOUR BRILLIANT LIFE

Examples include a well-known study of basketball players who over a six-week period of fifteen practice sessions were split into four groups with varying preparation routines. The group who undertook five minutes of relaxation and five minutes of guided Visualization prior to the practice session showed a statistically significant improvement at the end of the training period over the other three groups.

Kolonay, B. J. '*The Effects of Visuo-Motor Behaviour Rehearsal on Athletic Performance.*' Thesis, Hunter College, Dept. of Psychology, 1977.

A further example of the physical influence of Visualization is provided by an experiment carried out in 1992 by Dr Kelly Cole and Dr Guang Yue which showed a 22 per cent increase in muscle strength of a group of people performing a set of exercises in their imagination five times a week for four weeks. This compared with a 30 percent increase for the group who physically performed the exercises.

Yue, G. & Cole, K. J. 'Strength Increases from the Motor Programme: Comparison of Training with Maximal Voluntary and Imagined Muscle Contractions,' *Journal of Neurophysiology 67(5)*, pp. 1114-23. As cited in Pratt, G. and Lambrou, P. *Code To Joy*, 2012, Harper Collins, p.135 and Doidge, N. *The Brain That Changes Itself*, Penguin, 2007, p.204

Pham L. B. & Taylor S. E. 'From Thought to Action: Effects of Process – Versus Outcome – Based Mental Stimulations on Performance,' *Personality & Social Psychology Bulletin*, Feb 1999, Vol 25 no.2.

Oettingen G. & Mayer D. 'The motivating function of thinking about the future: Expectations versus fantasies.' *Journal of Personality & Social Psychology*, Vol 83 (5), Nov 2002 pp.1198-1212

Libby, L.K., Shaeffer, E.M., Eibach, R.P. & Slemmer, J.A. (2007) 'Picture yourself at the polls. Visual perspective in mental imager affects self-perception and behaviour. *Psychological Science*, 18, 199-203.

STEP 6. APPRECIATION

Coelho, P. *Manuscript found in Accra*, p.129

This position on the use of the word 'appreciation' is similar to that taken by Esther and Jerry Hicks, their version of the appreciation list is to create a book of positive aspects, Hicks, E. & Hicks, J. *Money and the Law of Attraction*, Hay House Ltd, 2008, pp.198-200

STEP 7. MINDFUL MEDITATION

Lewis Carroll, *Through the Looking Glass, and What Alice Found There*, 1871

It has been difficult to verify the author of this saying. Some sources quote Joan Rivers as the originator but I cannot say this is so with any certainty.

Barnes PM, Bloom B, Nahin R. Complementary and alternative medicine use among adults and children: United States, 2007. Center for Disease Control National Health Statistics Report #12. 2008.

A 2007 national Government survey that asked about CAM use in a sample of 23,393 U.S. adults found that 9.4 per cent of respondents (representing more than 20 million people) had used meditation in the past 12 months—compared with 7.6 per cent of respondents (representing more than 15 million people) in a similar survey conducted in 2002.

BBC, Horizon, *The Creative Brain: How Insight Works,* First shown in the UK 14th March 2013 on BBC2 .

Scientists trying to work out how moments of insights occur have found that there is a pause in the activity of the pre frontal cortex just prior to that flash of insight or inspiration happening. It is also noted in the programme that this lessening of pre frontal cortex activity can be purposefully induced through activity such as meditation.

WHAT NEXT?

Coelho, P. *Manuscript found in Accra,* p.129

11517311R00111

Printed in Great Britain
by Amazon.co.uk, Ltd.,
Marston Gate.